OUR KNOWLEDGE OF THE
EXTERNAL WORLD

BY BERTRAND RUSSELL

1896 *German Social Democracy*
1897 *An Essay on the Foundations of Geometry* (Constable)
1900 *The Philosophy of Leibniz*
1903 *The Principles of Mathematics*
1910 *Philosophical Essays*
1912 *Problems of Philosophy* (Oxford U.P.)
1910–13 *Principia Mathematica* 3 vols. (with A. N. Whitehead) (Cambridge U.P.)
1814 *Our Knowledge of the External World*
1816 *Justice in Wartime* (out of print)
1916 *Principles of Social Reconstruction*
1817 *Political Ideals*
1918 *Roads to Freedom*
1918 *Mysticism and Logic*
1919 *Introduction to Mathematical Philosophy*
1920 *The Practice and Theory of Bolshevism*
1921 *The Analysis of Mind*
1922 *The Problem of China*
1923 *Prospects of Industrial Civilization* (with Dora Russell)
1923 *The ABC of Atoms* (out of print)
1924 *Icarus or the Future of Science* (USA only)
1925 *The ABC of Relativity*
1925 *What I Believe*
1926 *On Education*
1927 *An Outline of Philosophy*
1927 *The Analysis of Matter*
1928 *Sceptical Essays*
1929 *Marriage and Morals*
1930 *The Conquest of Happiness*
1931 *The Scientific Outlook*
1932 *Education and the Social Order*
1934 *Freedom and Organization: 1814–1914*
1935 *In Praise of Idleness*
1935 *Religion and Science* (Oxford U.P.)
1936 *Which Way to Peace* (out of print)
1937 *The Amberley Papers* (with Patricia Russell)
1938 *Power*

1940 *An Inquiry into Meaning and Truth*
1945 *History of Western Philosophy*
1948 *Human Knowledge: Its Scope and Limits*
1949 *Authority and the Individual*
1950 *Unpopular Essays*
1951 *New Hopes for a Changing World*
1952 *The Impact of Science on Society*
1953 *The Good Citizen's Alphabet* (Gabberbochus)
1953 *Satan in the Suburbs*
1954 *Nightmares of Eminent Persons*
1954 *Human Society in Ethics and Politics*
1956 *Logic and Knowledge* (ed. by R. C. Marsh)
1956 *Portraits from Memory*
1957 *Why I am Not a Christian* (ed. by Paul Edwards)
1957 *Understanding History and other essays* (USA only)
1958 *Vital Letters of Russell, Khrushchev and Dulles* (Macgibbon & Kee)
1958 *Bertrand Russell's Best* (ed. by Robert Egner)
1959 *Common Sense and Nuclear Warfare*
1959 *Wisdom of the West* (ed. by Paul Foulkes) (Macdonald)
1959 *My Philosophical Development*
1960 *Bertrand Russell Speaks his Mind* (USA only)
1961 *Fact and Fiction*
1961 *Has Man a Future?*
1961 *The Basic Writings of Bertrand Russell* (ed. by R. E. Egner & L. Dennon)
1963 *Unarmed Victory*
1967 *War Crimes in Vietnam*
1967 *The Archives of Bertrand Russell* (ed. by B. Feinberg, Continuum) (out of print)
1967 *Autobiography 1872–1914*
1968 *Autobiography 1914–1944*
1969 *Autobiography 1944–1967*
1969 *Dear Bertrand Russell . . .* (ed. by B. Feinberg & R. Kasrils)
1972 *The Collected Stories of Bertrand Russell* (ed. by B. Feinberg)

BERTRAND RUSSELL

OUR KNOWLEDGE
OF THE
EXTERNAL WORLD

AS A FIELD FOR SCIENTIFIC
METHOD IN PHILOSOPHY

London
GEORGE ALLEN & UNWIN LTD
RUSKIN HOUSE MUSEUM STREET

First published in 1914 by
The Open Court Publishing Company
Reissued by George Allen & Unwin Ltd.
1922

Revised and reset 1926
Second impression 1949
Third impression 1952
Fourth impression 1961
Fifth impression 1969
Sixth impression 1972

ISBN 0 04 121008 5

Printed in Great Britain by
Unwin Brothers Ltd., Woking and London

PREFACE

THE following lectures [1] are an attempt to show, by means of examples, the nature, capacity, and limitations of the logical-analytic method in philosophy. This method, of which the first complete example is to be found in the writings of Frege, has gradually, in the course of actual research, increasingly forced itself upon me as something perfectly definite, capable of embodiment in maxims, and adequate, in all branches of philosophy, to yield whatever objective scientific knowledge it is possible to obtain. Most of the methods hitherto practised have professed to lead to more ambitious results than any that logical analysis can claim to reach, but unfortunately these results have always been such as many competent philosophers considered inadmissible. Regarded merely as hypotheses and as aids to imagination, the great systems of the past serve a very useful purpose, and are abundantly worthy of study. But something different is required if philosophy is to become a science, and to aim at results independent of the tastes and temperament of the philosopher who advocates them. In what follows, I have endeavoured to show, however imperfectly, the way by which I believe that this *desideratum* is to be found.

The central problem by which I have sought to illustrate method is the problem of the relation between the crude data of sense and the space, time, and matter

[1] Delivered as Lowell Lectures in Boston, in March and April, 1914.

of mathematical physics.   I have been made aware of the importance of this problem by my friend and collaborator Dr. Whitehead, to whom are due almost all the differences between the views advocated here and those suggested in *The Problems of Philosophy*.[1] I owe to him the definition of points, the suggestion for the treatment of instants and " things," and the whole conception of the world of physics as a *construction* rather than an *inference*.   What is said on these topics here is, in fact, a rough preliminary account of the more precise results which he is giving in the fourth volume of our *Principia Mathematica*.[2]   It will be seen that if his way of dealing with these topics is capable of being successfully carried through, a wholly new light is thrown on the time-honoured controversies of realists and idealists, and a method is obtained of solving all that is soluble in their problem.

The speculations of the past as to the reality or unreality of the world of physics were baffled, at the outset, by the absence of any satisfactory theory of the mathematical infinite.   This difficulty has been removed by the work of Georg Cantor.   But the positive and detailed solution of the problem by means of mathematical constructions based upon sensible objects as data has only been rendered possible by the growth of mathematical logic, without which it is practically impossible to manipulate ideas of the requisite abstractness and complexity.   This aspect, which is somewhat obscured in a merely popular outline such as is contained in the following lectures, will become plain as soon as Dr. Whitehead's work is published.   In pure logic, which, however, will be very

[1] London and New York, 1912 (" Home University Library ").
[2] The first volume was published at Cambridge in 1910, the second in 1912, and the third in 1913.

briefly discussed in these lectures, I have had the benefit of vitally important discoveries, not yet published, by my friend Mr. Ludwig Wittgenstein.

Since my purpose was to illustrate method, I have included much that is tentative and incomplete, for it is not by the study of finished structures alone that the manner of construction can be learnt. Except in regard to such matters as Cantor's theory of infinity, no finality is claimed for the theories suggested ; but I believe that where they are found to require modification, this will be discovered by substantially the same method as that which at present makes them appear probable, and it is on this ground that I ask the reader to be tolerant of their incompleteness.

CAMBRIDGE,
June 1914.

CONTENTS

OUR KNOWLEDGE OF THE EXTERNAL WORLD

LECTURE I

CURRENT TENDENCIES

PHILOSOPHY, from the earliest times, has made greater claims, and achieved fewer results, than any other branch of learning. Ever since Thales said that all is water, philosophers have been ready with glib assertions about the sum-total of things ; and equally glib denials have come from other philosophers ever since Thales was contradicted by Anaximander. I believe that the time has now arrived when this unsatisfactory state of things can be brought to an end. In the following course of lectures I shall try, chiefly by taking certain special problems as examples, to indicate wherein the claims of philosophers have been excessive, and why their achievements have not been greater. The problems and the method of philosophy have, I believe, been misconceived by all schools, many of its traditional problems being insoluble with our means of knowledge, while other more neglected but not less important problems can, by a more patient and more adequate method, be solved with all the precision and certainty to which the most advanced sciences have attained.

Among present-day philosophies, we may distinguish three principal types, often combined in varying proportions by a single philosopher, but in essence and tendency distinct. The first of these, which I shall call the classical tradition, descends in the main from Kant and Hegel; it represents the attempt to adapt to present needs the methods and results of the great constructive philosophers from Plato downwards. The second type, which may be called evolutionism, derived its predominance from Darwin, and must be reckoned as having had Herbert Spencer for its first philosophical representative; but in recent times it has become, chiefly through William James and M. Bergson, far bolder and far more searching in its innovations than it was in the hands of Herbert Spencer. The third type, which may be called " logical atomism " for want of a better name, has gradually crept into philosophy through the critical scrutiny of mathematics. This type of philosophy, which is the one that I wish to advocate, has not as yet many whole-hearted adherents, but the " new realism " which owes its inception to Harvard is very largely impregnated with its spirit. It represents, I believe, the same kind of advance as was introduced into physics by Galileo : the substitution of piecemeal, detailed, and verifiable results for large untested generalities recommended only by a certain appeal to imagination. But before we can understand the changes advocated by this new philosophy, we must briefly examine and criticize the other two types with which it has to contend.

A. THE CLASSICAL TRADITION

Twenty years ago, the classical tradition, having vanquished the opposing tradition of the English empiricists, held almost unquestioned sway in all Anglo-Saxon universities. At the present day, though it is losing ground, many of the most prominent teachers still adhere to it. In academic France, in spite of M. Bergson, it is far stronger than all its opponents combined ; and in Germany it had many vigorous advocates. Nevertheless, it represents on the whole a decaying force, and it has failed to adapt itself to the temper of the age. Its advocates are, in the main, those whose extra-philosophical knowledge is literary, rather than those who have felt the inspiration of science. There are, apart from reasoned arguments, certain general intellectual forces against it—the same general forces which are breaking down the other great syntheses of the past, and making our age one of bewildered grouping where our ancestors walked in the clear daylight of unquestioning certainty.

The original impulse out of which the classical tradition developed was the naïve faith of the Greek philosophers in the omnipotence of reasoning. The discovery of geometry had intoxicated them, and its *a priori* deductive method appeared capable of universal application. They would prove, for instance, that all reality is one, that there is no such thing as change, that the world of sense is a world of mere illusion ; and the strangeness of their results gave them no qualms because they believed in the correctness of their reasoning. Thus it came to be thought that by mere thinking the most surprising and important truths concerning the whole of reality could be established with a certainty which no contrary observations could shake. As the vital impulse of the early philosophers died away, its place was taken by authority and tradition, reinforced, in the Middle Ages and almost to our own day, by systematic theology.

Modern philosophy, from Descartes onwards, though not bound by authority like that of the Middle Ages, still accepted more or less uncritically the Aristotelian logic. Moreover, it still believed, except in Great Britain, that *a priori* reasoning could reveal otherwise undiscoverable secrets about the universe, and could prove reality to be quite different from what, to direct observation, it appears to be. It is this belief, rather than any particular tenets resulting from it, that I regard as the distinguishing characteristic of the classical tradition, and as hitherto the main obstacle to a scientific attitude in philosophy.

The nature of the philosophy embodied in the classical tradition may be made clearer by taking a particular exponent as an illustration. For this purpose, let us consider for a moment the doctrines of Mr. Bradley, who is probably the most distinguished British representative of this school. Mr. Bradley's *Appearance and Reality* is a book consisting of two parts, the first called *Appearance*, the second *Reality*. The first part examines and condemns almost all that makes up our everyday world : things and qualities, relations, space and time, change, causation, activity, the self. All these, though in some sense facts which qualify reality, are not real as they appear. What is real is one single, indivisible, timeless whole, called the Absolute, which is in some sense spiritual, but does not consist of souls, or of thought and will as we know them. And all this is established by abstract logical reasoning professing to find self-contradictions in the categories condemned as mere appearance, and to leave no tenable alternative to the kind of Absolute which is finally affirmed to be real.

One brief example may suffice to illustrate Mr. Bradley's method. The world appears to be full of many things with various relations to each other—right and left, before and after, father and son, and so on. But relations, according to Mr. Bradley, are found on examination to be self-contradictory and therefore impossible. He first argues that, if there are relations, there must be qualities between which they hold. This part of his argument need not detain us. He then proceeds :

" But how the relation can stand to the qualities is, on the other side, unintelligible. If it is nothing to the qualities, then they are not related at all ; and, if so, as we saw, they have ceased to be qualities, and their relation is a nonentity. But if it is to be something to them, then clearly we shall require a *new* connecting relation. For the relation hardly can be the mere adjective of one or both of its terms ; or, at least, as such it seems indefensible. And, being something itself, if it does not itself bear a relation to the terms, in what intelligible way will it succeed in being anything to them ? But here again we are hurried off into the eddy of a hopeless process, since we are forced to go on finding new relations without end. The links are united by a link, and this bond of union is a link which also has two ends ; and these require each a fresh link to connect them with the old. The problem is to find how the relation can stand to its qualities, and this problem is insoluble." [1]

I do not propose to examine this argument in detail, or to show the exact points where, in my opinion, it is fallacious. I have quoted it only as an example of method. Most people will admit, I think, that it is calculated to produce bewilderment rather than conviction, because there is more likelihood of error

[1] *Appearance and Reality*, pp. 32–33.

in a very subtle, abstract, and difficult argument than in so patent a fact as the interrelatedness of the things in the world. To the early Greeks, to whom geometry was practically the only known science, it was possible to follow reasoning with assent even when it led to the strangest conclusions. But to us, with our methods of experiment and observation, our knowledge of the long history of *a priori* errors refuted by empirical science, it has become natural to suspect a fallacy in any deduction of which the conclusion appears to contradict patent facts. It is easy to carry such suspicion too far, and it is very desirable, if possible, actually to discover the exact nature of the error when it exists. But there is no doubt that what we may call the empirical outlook has become part of most educated people's habit of mind ; and it is this, rather than any definite argument, that has diminished the hold of the classical tradition upon students of philosophy and the instructed public generally.

The function of logic in philosophy, as I shall try to show at a later stage, is all-important ; but I do not think its function is that which it has in the classical tradition. In that tradition, logic becomes constructive through negation. Where a number of alternatives seem, at first sight, to be equally possible, logic is made to condemn all of them except one, and that one is then pronounced to be realized in the actual world. Thus the world is constructed by means of logic, with little or no appeal to concrete experience. The true function of logic is, in my opinion, exactly the opposite of this. As applied to matters of experience, it is analytic rather than constructive ; taken *a priori*, it shows the possibility of hitherto unsuspected alternatives more often than the impossibility

of alternatives which seemed *prima facie* possible.
Thus, while it liberates imagination as to what the
world *may* be, it refuses to legislate as to what the
world *is*. This change, which has been brought about
by an internal revolution in logic, has swept away the
ambitious constructions of traditional metaphysics,
even for those whose faith in logic is greatest ; while
to the many who regard logic as a chimera the paradoxical systems to which it has given rise do not seem
worthy even of refutation. Thus on all sides these
systems have ceased to attract, and even the philosophical world tends more and more to pass them by.

One or two of the favourite doctrines of the school
we are considering may be mentioned to illustrate
the nature of its claims. The universe, it tells us, is
an " organic unity," like an animal or a perfect work
of art. By this it means, roughly speaking, that all
the different parts fit together and co-operate, and
are what they are because of their place in the whole.
This belief is sometimes advanced dogmatically,
while at other times it is defended by certain logical
arguments. If it is true, every part of the universe
is a microcosm, a miniature reflection of the whole.
If we knew ourselves thoroughly, according to this
doctrine, we should know everything. Common sense
would naturally object that there are people—say
in China—with whom our relations are so indirect
and trivial that we cannot infer anything important
as to them from any fact about ourselves. If there
are living beings in Mars or in more distant parts of
the universe, the same argument becomes even stronger.
But further, perhaps the whole contents of the space
and time in which we live form only one of many
universes, each seeming to itself complete. And thus
the conception of the necessary unity of all that is

resolves itself into the poverty of imagination, and a freer logic emancipates us from the strait-waistcoated benevolent institution which idealism palms off as the totality of being.

Another very important doctrine held by most, though not all, of the school we are examining is the doctrine that all reality is what is called " mental " or " spiritual," or that, at any rate, all reality is dependent for its existence upon what is mental. This view is often particularized into the form which states that the relation of knower and known is fundamental, and that nothing can exist unless it either knows or is known. Here again the same legislative function is ascribed to *a priori* argumentation : it is thought that there are contradictions in an unknown reality. Again, if I am not mistaken, the argument is fallacious, and a better logic will show that no limits can be set to the extent and nature of the unknown. And when I speak of the unknown, I do not mean merely what we personally do not know, but what is not known to any mind. Here as elsewhere, while the older logic shut out possibilities and imprisoned imagination within the walls of the familiar, the newer logic shows rather what may happen, and refuses to decide as to what *must* happen.

The classical tradition in philosophy is the last surviving child of two very diverse parents : the Greek belief in reason, and the mediæval belief in the tidiness of the universe. To the schoolmen, who lived amid wars, massacres, and pestilences, nothing appeared so delightful as safety and order. In their idealizing dreams, it was safety and order that they sought : the universe of Thomas Aquinas or Dante is as small and neat as a Dutch interior. To us, to whom safety has become monotony, to whom the primeval savageries of nature are so remote as to become a mere pleasing condiment to our ordered routine, the world of dreams is very different from what it was amid the wars of Guelf and Ghibelline. Hence William James's protest against what he calls the " block universe " of the classical tradition ; hence Nietzsche's worship of force ; hence the verbal bloodthirstiness of many quiet literary men. The barbaric substratum of human nature, unsatisfied in action, finds an outlet in imagination. In philosophy, as elsewhere, this tendency is visible ; and it is this, rather than formal argument, that has thrust aside the classical tradition for a philosophy which fancies itself more virile and more vital.[1]

B. EVOLUTIONISM

Evolutionism, in one form or another, is the prevailing creed of our time. It dominates our politics, our literature, and not least our philosophy. Nietzsche, pragmatism, Bergson, are phases in its philosophic development, and their popularity far beyond the circles of professional philosophers shows its consonance with the spirit of the age. It believes itself firmly based on science, a liberator of hopes, an inspirer of an invigorating faith in human power, a sure antidote to the ratiocinative authority of the Greeks and the dogmatic authority of mediæval systems. Against so fashionable and so agreeable a creed it may seem useless to raise a protest ; and with much of its spirit every modern man must be in sympathy. But I think that, in the intoxication of a quick success, much that is important, and vital to a true understanding of the universe has been forgotten. Something of Hellenism

[1] Written before August 1914.

must be combined with the new spirit before it can emerge from the ardour of youth into the wisdom of manhood. And it is time to remember that biology is neither the only science, nor yet the model to which all other sciences must adapt themselves. Evolutionism, as I shall try to show, is not a truly scientific philosophy, either in its method or in the problems which it considers. The true scientific philosophy is something more arduous and more aloof, appealing to less mundane hopes, and requiring a severer discipline for its successful practice.

Darwin's *Origin of Species* persuaded the world that the difference between different species of animals and plants is not the fixed, immutable difference that it appears to be. The doctrine of natural kinds, which had rendered classification easy and definite, which was enshrined in the Aristotelian tradition, and protected by its supposed necessity for orthodox dogma, was suddenly swept away for ever out of the biological world. The difference between man and the lower animals, which to our human conceit appears enormous, was shown to be a gradual achievement, involving intermediate beings who could not with certainty be placed either within or without the human family. The sun and planets had already been shown by Laplace to be very probably derived from a primitive more or less undifferentiated nebula. Thus the old fixed landmarks became wavering and indistinct, and all sharp outlines were blurred. Things and species lost their boundaries, and none could say where they began or where they ended.

But if human conceit was staggered for a moment by its kinship with the ape, it soon found a way to reassert itself, and that way is the " philosophy " of evolution. A process which led from the amœba to man appeared to the philosophers to be obviously a progress—though whether the amœba would agree with this opinion is not known. Hence the cycle of changes which science had shown to be the probable history of the past was welcomed as revealing a law of development towards good in the universe—an evolution or unfolding of an ideal slowly embodying itself in the actual. But such a view, though it might satisfy Spencer and those whom we may call Hegelian evolutionists, could not be accepted as adequate by the more whole-hearted votaries of change. An ideal to which the world continuously approaches is, to these minds, too dead and static to be inspiring. Not only the aspirations, but the ideal too, must change and develop with the course of evolution ; there must be no fixed goal, but a continual fashioning of fresh needs by the impulse which is life and which alone gives unity to the process.

Ever since the seventeenth century, those whom William James described as the " tender-minded " have been engaged in a desperate struggle with the mechanical view of the course of nature which physical science seems to impose. A great part of the attractiveness of the classical tradition was due to the partial escape from mechanism which it provided. But now, with the influence of biology, the " tender-minded " believe that a more radical escape is possible, sweeping aside not merely the laws of physics, but the whole apparently immutable apparatus of logic, with its fixed concepts, its general principles, and its reasonings which seem able to compel even the most unwilling assent. The older kind of teleology, therefore, which regarded the End as a fixed goal, already partially visible, towards which we were gradually approaching, is rejected by M. Bergson as not allowing enough for the absolute dominion of change. After explaining why he does not accept mechanism, he proceeds : [1]

" But radical finalism is quite as unacceptable, and for the same reason. The doctrine of teleology, in its extreme form, as we find it in Leibniz for example, implies that things and beings merely realize a programme previously arranged. But if there is nothing unforeseen, no invention or creation in the universe, time is useless again. As in the mechanistic hypothesis, here again it is supposed that *all is given*. Finalism thus understood is only inverted mechanism. It springs from the same postulate, with this sole difference, that in the movement of our finite intellects along successive things, whose successiveness is reduced to a mere appearance, it holds in front of us the light with which it claims to guide us, instead of putting it behind. It substitutes the attraction of the future for the impulsion of the past. But succession remains none the less a mere appearance, as indeed does movement itself. In the doctrine of Leibniz, time is reduced to a confused perception, relative to the human standpoint, a perception which would vanish, like a rising mist, for a mind seated at the centre of things.

" Yet finalism is not, like mechanism, a doctrine with fixed rigid outlines. It admits of as many inflections as we like. The mechanistic philosophy is to be taken or left : it must be left if the least grain of dust, by straying from the path foreseen by mechanics, should show the slightest trace of spontaneity. The doctrine of final causes, on the contrary, will never be definitively refuted. If one form of it be put aside, it will take another. Its principle, which is essentially psychological, is very flexible. It is so extensible, and thereby so comprehensive, that one accepts some-

[1] *Creative Evolution*, English translation, p. 41.

thing of it as soon as one rejects pure mechanism. The theory we shall put forward in this book will therefore necessarily partake of finalism to a certain extent."

M. Bergson's form of finalism depends upon his conception of life. Life, in his philosophy, is a continuous stream, in which all divisions are artificial and unreal. Separate things, beginnings and endings, are mere convenient fictions : there is only smooth, unbroken transition. The beliefs of to-day may count as true to-day, if they carry us along the stream ; but to-morrow they will be false, and must be replaced by new beliefs to meet the new situation. All our thinking consists of convenient fictions, imaginary congealings of the stream : reality flows on in spite of all our fictions, and though it can be lived, it cannot be conceived in thought. Somehow, without explicit statement, the assurance is slipped in that the future, though we cannot foresee it, will be better than the past or the present : the reader is like the child who expects a sweet because it has been told to open its mouth and shut its eyes. Logic, mathematics, physics, disappear in this philosophy, because they are too " static " ; what is real is an impulse and movement towards a goal which, like the rainbow, recedes as we advance, and makes every place different when we reach it from what it appeared to be at a distance.

Now I do not propose at present to enter upon a technical examination of this philosophy. At present I wish to make only two criticisms of it—first, that its truth does not follow from what science has rendered probable concerning the facts of evolution, and secondly, that the motives and interests which inspire it are so exclusively practical, and the problems with which it deals are so special, that it can hardly be regarded as really touching any of the questions that to my mind constitute genuine philosophy.

(1) What biology has rendered probable is that the diverse species arose by adaptation from a less differentiated ancestry. This fact is in itself exceedingly interesting, but it is not the kind of fact from which philosophical consequences follow. Philosophy is general, and takes an impartial interest in all that exists. The changes suffered by minute portions of matter on the earth's surface are very important to us as active sentient beings ; but to us as philosophers they have no greater interest than other changes in portions of matter elsewhere. And if the changes on the earth's surface during the last few millions of years appear to our present ethical notions to be in the nature of a progress, that gives no ground for believing that progress is a general law of the universe. Except under the influence of desire, no one would admit for a moment so crude a generalization from such a tiny selection of facts. What does result, not specially from biology, but from all the sciences which deal with what exists, is that we cannot understand the world unless we can understand change and continuity. This is even more evident in physics than it is in biology. But the analysis of change and continuity is not a problem upon which either physics or biology throws any light : it is a problem of a new kind, belonging to a different kind of study. The question whether evolutionism offers a true or a false answer to this problem is not, therefore, a question to be solved by appeals to particular facts, such as biology and physics reveal. In assuming dogmatically a certain answer to this question, evolutionism ceases to be scientific, yet it is only in touching on this question that evolutionism reaches the subject-matter of philo-

sophy. Evolutionism thus consists of two parts : one not philosophical, but only a hasty generalization of the kind which the special sciences might hereafter confirm or confute ; the other not scientific, but a mere unsupported dogma, belonging to philosophy by its subject-matter, but in no way deducible from the facts upon which evolutionism relies.

(2) The predominant interest of evolutionism is in the question of human destiny, or at least of the destiny of Life. It is more interested in morality and happiness than in knowledge for its own sake. It must be admitted that the same may be said of many other philosophies, and that a desire for the kind of knowledge which philosophy really can give is very rare. But if philosophy is to become scientific —and it is our object to discover how this can be achieved—it is necessary first and foremost that philosophers should acquire the disinterested intellectual curiosity which characterizes the genuine man of science. Knowledge concerning the future—which is the kind of knowledge that must be sought if we are to know about human destiny—is possible within certain narrow limits. It is impossible to say how much the limits may be enlarged with the progress of science. But what is evident is that any proposition about the future belongs by its subject-matter to some particular science, and is to be ascertained, if at all, by the methods of that science. Philosophy is not a short cut to the same kind of results as those of the other sciences : if it is to be a genuine study, it must have a province of its own, and aim at results which the other sciences can neither prove nor disprove.

The consideration that philosophy, if there is such a study, must consist of propositions which could not occur in the other sciences, is one which has very

far-reaching consequences. All the questions which
have what is called a human interest—such, for
example, as the question of a future life—belong, at
least in theory, to special sciences, and are capable,
at least in theory, of being decided by empirical
evidence. Philosophers have too often, in the past,
permitted themselves to pronounce on empirical
questions, and found themselves, as a result, in dis-
astrous conflict with well-attested facts. We must,
therefore, renounce the hope that philosophy can
promise satisfaction to our mundane desires. What
it can do, when it is purified from all practical taint,
is to help us to understand the general aspects of the
world and the logical analysis of familiar but complex
things. Through this achievement, by the suggestion
of fruitful hypotheses, it may be indirectly useful in
other sciences, notably mathematics, physics, and
psychology. But a genuinely scientific philosophy
cannot hope to appeal to any except those who have
the wish to understand, to escape from intellectual
bewilderment. It offers, in its own domain, the kind
of satisfaction which the other sciences offer. But
it does not offer, or attempt to offer, a solution of the
problem of human destiny, or of the destiny of the
universe.

Evolutionism, if what has been said is true, is to be
regarded as a hasty generalization from certain rather
special facts, accompanied by a dogmatic rejection
of all attempts at analysis, and inspired by interests
which are practical rather than theoretical. In spite,
therefore, of its appeal to detailed results in various
sciences, it cannot be regarded as any more genuinely
scientific than the classical tradition which it has
replaced. How philosophy is to be rendered scientific,
and what is the true subject-matter of philosophy,

I shall try to show first by examples of certain achieved results, and then more generally. We will begin with the problem of the physical conceptions of space and time and matter, which, as we have seen, are challenged by the contentions of the evolutionists. That these conceptions stand in need of reconstruction will be admitted, and is indeed increasingly urged by physicists themselves. It will also be admitted that the reconstruction must take more account of change and the universal flux than is done in the older mechanics with its fundamental conception of an indestructible matter. But I do not think the reconstruction required is on Bergsonian lines, nor do I think that his rejection of logic can be anything but harmful. I shall not, however, adopt the method of explicit controversy, but rather the method of independent inquiry, starting from what, in a pre-philosophic stage, appear to be facts, and keeping always as close to these initial data as the requirements of consistency will permit.

Although explicit controversy is almost always fruitless in philosophy, owing to the fact that no two philosophers ever understand one another, yet it seems necessary to say something at the outset in justification of the scientific as against the mystical attitude. Metaphysics, from the first, has been developed by the union or the conflict of these two attitudes. Among the earliest Greek philosophers, the Ionians were more scientific, and the Sicilians more mystical.[1] But among the latter, Pythagoras, for example, was in himself a curious mixture of the two tendencies : the scientific attitude led him to his proposition on right-angled triangles, while his mystic insight showed him that it is wicked to eat beans.

[1] Cf. Burnet, *Early Greek Philosophy*, pp. 85 ff.

Naturally enough, his followers divided into two sects, the lovers of right-angled triangles and the abhorrers of beans ; but the former sect died out, leaving, however, a haunting flavour of mysticism over much Greek mathematical speculation, and in particular over Plato's views on mathematics. Plato, of course, embodies both the scientific and mystical attitudes in a higher form than his predecessors, but the mystical attitude is distinctly the stronger of the two, and secures ultimate victory whenever the conflict is sharp. Plato, moreover, adopted from the Eleatics the device of using logic to defeat common sense, and thus to leave the field clear for mysticism— a device still employed in our own day by the adherents of the classical tradition.

The logic used in defence of mysticism seems to me faulty as logic, and in a later lecture I shall criticize it on this ground. But the more thoroughgoing mystics do not employ logic, which they despise : they appeal instead directly to the immediate deliverance of their insight. Now, although fully developed mysticism is rare in the West, some tincture of it colours the thoughts of many people, particularly as regards matter on which they have strong convictions not based on evidence. In all who seek passionately for the fugitive and difficult goods, the conviction is almost irresistible that there is in the world something deeper, more significant, than the multiplicity of little facts chronicled and classified by science. Behind the veil of these mundane things, they feel something quite different obscurely shimmers, shining forth clearly in the great moments of illumination, which alone give anything worthy to be called real knowledge of truth. To seek such moments, therefore, is to them the way of wisdom, rather than, like the man of science, to observe coolly, to analyse without emotion, and to accept without question the equal reality of the trivial and the important.

Of the reality or unreality of the mystic's world I know nothing. I have no wish to deny it, nor even to declare that the insight which reveals it is not a genuine insight. What I do wish to maintain— and it is here that the scientific attitude becomes imperative—is that insight, untested and unsupported, is an insufficient guarantee of truth, in spite of the fact that much of the most important truth is first suggested by its means. It is common to speak of an opposition between instinct and reason ; in the eighteenth century, the opposition was drawn in favour of reason, but under the influence of Rousseau and the romantic movement instinct was given the preference, first by those who rebelled against artificial forms of government and thought, and then, as the purely rationalistic defence of traditional theology became increasingly difficult, by all who felt in science a menace to creeds which they associated with a spiritual outlook on life and the world. Bergson, under the name of " intuition," has raised instinct to the position of sole arbiter of metaphysical truth. But in fact the opposition of instinct and reason is mainly illusory. Instinct, intuition, or insight is what first leads to the beliefs which subsequent reason confirms or confutes ; but the confirmation, where it is possible, consists, in the last analysis, of agreement with other beliefs no less instinctive. Reason is a harmonizing, controlling force rather than a creative one. Even in the most purely logical realms, it is insight that first arrives at what is new.

Where instinct and reason do sometimes conflict is in regard to single beliefs, held instinctively, and

held with such determination that no degree of inconsistency with other beliefs leads to their abandon-
ment. Instinct, like all human faculties, is liable to
error Those in whom reason is weak are often unwilling to admit this as regards themselves, though
all admit it in regard to others. Where instinct is
least liable to error is in practical matters as to which
right judgment is a help to survival ; friendship
and hostility in others, for instance, are often felt
with extraordinary discrimination through very care-
ful disguises. But even in such matters a wrong impression may be given by reserve or flattery ; and
in matters less directly practical, such as philosophy
deals with, very strong instinctive beliefs may be
wholly mistaken, as we may come to know through
their perceived inconsistency with other equally
strong beliefs. It is such considerations that necessitate the harmonizing mediation of reason, which
tests our beliefs by their mutual compatibility, and
examines, in doubtful cases, the possible sources of
error on the one side and on the other. In this there
is no opposition to instinct as a whole, but only to
blind reliance upon some one interesting aspect of
instinct to the exclusion of other more commonplace
but not less trustworthy aspects. It is such one-
sidedness, not instinct itself, that reason aims at
correcting.

These more or less trite maxims may be illustrated
by application to Bergson's advocacy of " intuition "
as against " intellect." There are, he says, " two
profoundly different ways of knowing a thing. The
first implies that we move round the object ; the
second that we enter into it. The first depends on
the point of view at which we are placed and on the
symbols by which we express ourselves. The second

neither depends on a point of view nor relies on any symbol. The first kind of knowledge may be said to stop at the *relative* ; the second, in those cases where it is possible, to attain the *absolute*." ¹ The second of these, which is intuition, is, he says, " the kind of intellectual *sympathy* by which one places oneself within an object in order to coincide with what is unique in it and therefore inexpressible " (p. 6). In illustration, he mentions self-knowledge : " there is one reality, at least, which we all seize from within, by intuition and not by simple analysis. It is our own personality in its flowing through time— our self which endures " (p. 8). The rest of Bergson's philosophy consists in reporting, through the imperfect medium of words, the knowledge gained by intuition, and the consequent complete condemnation of all the pretended knowledge derived from science and common sense.

This procedure, since it takes sides in a conflict of instinctive beliefs, stands in need of justification by proving the greater trustworthiness of the beliefs on one side than of those on the other. Bergson attempts this justification in two ways—first, by explaining that intellect is a purely practical faculty designed to secure biological success ; secondly, by mentioning remarkable feats of instinct in animals, and by pointing out characteristics of the world which, though intuition can apprehend them, are baffling to intellect as he interprets it.

Of Bergson's theory that intellect is a purely practical faculty developed in the struggle for survival, and not a source of true beliefs, we may say, first, that it is only through intellect that we know of the struggle for survival and of the biological ancestry of man : if

¹ *Introduction to Metaphysics*, p. 1.

3

the intellect is misleading, the whole of this merely inferred history is presumably untrue. If, on the other hand, we agree with M. Bergson in thinking that evolution took place as Darwin believed, then it is not only intellect, but all our faculties, that have been developed under the stress of practical utility. Intuition is seen at its best where it is directly useful—for example, in regard to other people's characters and dispositions. Bergson apparently holds that capacity for this kind of knowledge is less explicable by the struggle for existence than, for example, capacity for pure mathematics. Yet the savage deceived by false friendship is likely to pay for his mistake with his life ; whereas even in the most civilized societies men are not put to death for mathematical incompetence. All the most striking of his instances of intuition in animals have a very direct survival value. The fact is, of course, that both intuition and intellect have been developed because they are useful, and that, speaking broadly, they are useful when they give truth and become harmful when they give falsehood. Intellect, in civilized man, like artistic capacity, has occasionally been developed beyond the point where it is useful to the individual ; intuition, on the other hand, seems on the whole to diminish as civilization increases. Speaking broadly, it is greater in children than in adults, in the uneducated than in the educated. Probably in dogs it exceeds anything to be found in human beings. But those who find in these facts a recommendation of intuition ought to return to running wild in the woods, dyeing themselves with woad and living on hips and haws.

Let us next examine whether intuition possesses any such infallibility as Bergson claims for it. The best

instance of it, according to him, is our acquaintance
with ourselves ; yet self-knowledge is proverbially
rare and difficult. Most men, for example, have in
their nature meannesses, vanities, and envies of which
they are quite unconscious, though even their best
friends can perceive them without any difficulty. It
is true that intuition has a convincingness which is
lacking to intellect : while it is present, it is almost
impossible to doubt its truth. But if it should appear,
on examination, to be at least as fallible as intellect,
its greater subjective certainty becomes a demerit,
making it only the more irresistibly deceptive. Apart
from self-knowledge, one of the most notable examples
of intuition is the knowledge people believe themselves
to possess of those with whom they are in love : the
wall between different personalities seems to become
transparent, and people think they see into another
soul as into their own. Yet deception in such cases
is constantly practised with success ; and even where
there is no intentional deception, experience gradually
proves, as a rule, that the supposed insight was illusory,
and that the slower, more groping methods of the
intellect are in the long run more reliable.

Bergson maintains that intellect can only deal
with things in so far as they resemble what has been
experienced in the past, while intuition has the power
of apprehending the uniqueness and novelty that
always belong to each fresh moment. That there is
something unique and new at every moment, is certainly true ; it is also true that this cannot be fully
expressed by means of intellectual concepts. Only
direct acquaintance can give knowledge of what is
unique and new. But direct acquaintance of this
kind is given fully in sensation, and does not require,
so far as I can see, any special faculty of intuition for

its apprehension. It is neither intellect nor intuition, but sensation, that supplies new data ; but when the data are new in any remarkable manner, intellect is much more capable of dealing with them than intuition would be. The hen with a brood of ducklings no doubt has intuitions which seem to place her inside them, and not merely to know them analytically ; but when the ducklings take to the water, the whole apparent intuition is seen to be illusory, and the hen is left helpless on the shore. Intuition, in fact, is an aspect and development of instinct, and, like all instinct, is admirable in those customary surroundings which have moulded the habits of the animal in question, but totally incompetent as soon as the surroundings are changed in a way which demands some non-habitual mode of action.

The theoretical understanding of the world, which is the aim of philosophy, is not a matter of great practical importance to animals, or to savages, or even to most civilized men. It is hardly to be supposed, therefore, that the rapid, rough and ready methods of instinct or intuition will find in this field a favourable ground for their application. It is the older kinds of activity, which bring out our kinship with remote generations of animal and semi-human ancestors, that show intuition at its best. In such matters as self-preservation and love, intuition will act sometimes (though not always) with a swiftness and precision which are astonishing to the critical intellect. But philosophy is not one of the pursuits which illustrate our affinity with the past : it is a highly refined, highly civilized pursuit, demanding, for its success, a certain liberation from the life of instinct, and even, at times, a certain aloofness from all mundane hopes and fears. It is not in philosophy, therefore, that we can hope to see intuition at its best. On the contrary, since the true objects of philosophy, and the habits of thought demanded for their apprehension, are strange, unusual, and remote, it is here, more almost than anywhere else, that intellect proves superior to intuition, and that quick unanalysed convictions are least deserving of uncritical acceptance.

Before embarking upon the somewhat difficult and abstract discussions which lie before us, it will be well to take a survey of the hopes we may retain and the hopes we must abandon. The hope of satisfaction to our more human desires—the hope of demonstrating that the world has this or that desirable ethical characteristic—is not one which, so far as I can see, philosophy can do anything whatever to satisfy. The difference between a good world and a bad one is a difference in the particular characteristics of the particular things that exist in these worlds : it is not a sufficiently abstract difference to come within the province of philosophy. Love and hate, for example, are ethical opposites, but to philosophy they are closely analogous attitudes towards objects. The general form and structure of those attitudes towards objects which constitute mental phenomena is a problem for philosophy ; but the difference between love and hate is not a difference of form or structure, and therefore belongs rather to the special science of psychology than to philosophy. Thus the ethical interests which have often inspired philosophers must remain in the background : some kind of ethical interest may inspire the whole study, but none must obtrude in the detail or be expected in the special results which are sought.

If this view seems at first sight disappointing, we may remind ourselves that a similar change has been

found necessary in all the other sciences. The physicist or chemist is not now required to prove the ethical
importance of his ions or atoms ; the biologist is not
expected to prove the utility of the plants or animals
which he dissects. In pre-scientific ages this was not
the case. Astronomy, for example, was studied
because men believed in astrology : it was thought
that the movements of the planets had the most direct
and important bearing upon the lives of human beings.
Presumably, when this belief decayed and the disinterested study of astronomy began, many who had
found astrology absorbingly interesting decided that
astronomy had too little human interest to be worthy
of study. Physics, as it appears in Plato's *Timæus*
for example, is full of ethical notions : it is an essential
part of its purpose to show that the earth is worthy
of admiration. The modern physicist, on the contrary, though he has no wish to deny that the earth
is admirable, is not concerned, as physicist, with its
ethical tributes : he is merely concerned to find out
facts, not to consider whether they are good or bad.
In psychology, the scientific attitude is even more
recent and more difficult than in the physical sciences :
it is natural to consider that human nature is either
good or bad, and to suppose that the difference between
good and bad, so all-important in practice, must be
important in theory also. It is only during the last
century that an ethically neutral science of psychology
has grown up ; and here too ethical neutrality has
been essential to scientific success.

In philosophy, hitherto, ethical neutrality has been
seldom sought and hardly ever achieved. Men have
remembered their wishes, and have judged philosophies
in relation to their wishes. Driven from the particular sciences, the belief that the notions of good

and evil must afford a key to the understanding of the world has sought a refuge in philosophy. But even from this last refuge, if philosophy is not to remain a set of pleasing dreams, this belief must be driven forth. It is a commonplace that happiness is not best achieved by those who seek it directly ; and it would seem that the same is true of the good. In thought, at any rate, those who forget good and evil and seek only to know the facts are more likely to achieve good than those who view the world through the distorting medium of their own desires.

The immense extension of our knowledge of facts in recent times has had, as it had in the Renaissance, two effects upon the general intellectual outlook. On the one hand, it has made men distrustful of the truth of wide, ambitious systems : theories come and go swiftly, each serving, for a moment, to classify known facts and promote the search for new ones, but each in turn proving inadequate to deal with the new facts when they have been found. Even those who invent the theories do not, in science, regard them as anything but a temporary makeshift. The ideal of an all-embracing synthesis, such as the Middle Ages believed themselves to have attained, recedes further and further beyond the limits of what seems feasible. In such a world, as in the world of Montaigne, nothing seems worth while except the discovery of more and more facts, each in turn the death-blow to some cherished theory ; the ordering intellect grows weary, and becomes slovenly through despair.

On the other hand, the new facts have brought new powers ; man's physical control over natural forces has been increasing with unexampled rapidity, and promises to increase in the future beyond all easily assignable limits. Thus alongside of despair as regards ultimate theory there is an immense optimism as regards practice : what man can *do* seems almost boundless. The old fixed limits of human power, such as death, or the dependence of the race on an equilibrium of cosmic forces, are forgotten, and no hard facts are allowed to break in upon the dream of omnipotence. No philosophy is tolerated which sets bounds to man's capacity of gratifying his wishes ; and thus the very despair of theory is invoked to silence every whisper of doubt as regards the possibilities of practical achievement.

In the welcoming of new fact, and in the suspicion of dogmatism as regards the universe at large, the modern spirit should, I think, be accepted as wholly an advance. But both in its practical pretensions and in its theoretical despair it seems to me to go too far. Most of what is greatest in man is called forth in response to the thwarting of his hopes by immutable natural obstacles ; by the pretence of omnipotence, he becomes trivial and a little absurd. And on the theoretical side, ultimate metaphysical truth, though less all-embracing and harder of attainment than it appeared to some philosophers in the past, can, I believe, be discovered by those who are willing to combine the hopefulness, patience, and open-mindedness of science with something of the Greek feeling for beauty in the abstract world of logic and for the ultimate intrinsic value in the contemplation of truth.

The philosophy, therefore, which is to be genuinely inspired by the scientific spirit, must deal with somewhat dry and abstract matters, and must not hope to find an answer to the practical problems of life. To those who wish to understand much of what has in the past been most difficult and obscure in the constitution of the universe, it has great rewards to offer—triumphs as noteworthy as those of Newton and Darwin, and as important, in the long run, for the moulding of our mental habits. And it brings with it—as a new and powerful method of investigation always does—a sense of power and a hope of progress more reliable and better grounded than any that rests on hasty and fallacious generalization as to the nature of the universe at large. Many hopes which inspired philosophers in the past it cannot claim to fulfil; but other hopes, more purely intellectual, it can satisfy more fully than former ages could have deemed possible for human minds.

LECTURE II

LOGIC AS THE ESSENCE OF
PHILOSOPHY

THE topics we discussed in our first lecture, and the topics we shall discuss later, all reduce themselves, in so far as they are genuinely philosophical, to problems of logic. This is not due to any accident, but to the fact that every philosophical problem, when it is subjected to the necessary analysis and purification, is found either to be not really philosophical at all, or else to be, in the sense in which we are using the word, logical. But as the word " logic " is never used in the same sense by two different philosophers, some explanation of what I mean by the word is indispensable at the outset.

Logic, in the Middle Ages, and down to the present day in teaching, meant no more than a scholastic collection of technical terms and rules of syllogistic inference. Aristotle had spoken, and it was the part of humbler men merely to repeat the lesson after him. The trivial nonsense embodied in this tradition is still set in examinations, and defended by eminent authorities as an excellent " propædeutic," i.e. a training in those habits of solemn humbug which are so great a help in later life. But it is not this that I mean to praise in saying that all philosophy is logic. Ever since the beginning of the seventeenth century, all vigorous minds that have concerned themselves with inference have abandoned the mediæval tradition, and in one way or other have widened the scope of logic. The first extension was the introduction of the inductive method by Bacon and Galileo—by the former in a theoretical and largely mistaken form, by the latter in actual use in establishing the foundations of modern physics and astronomy. This is probably the only extension of the old logic which has become familiar to the general educated public. But induction, important as it is when regarded as a method of investigation, does not seem to remain when its work is done : in the final form of a perfected science, it would seem that everything ought to be deductive. If induction remains at all, which is a difficult question, it will remain merely as one of the principles according to which deductions are effected. Thus the ultimate result of the introduction of the inductive method seems not the creation of a new kind of non-deductive reasoning, but rather the widening of the scope of deduction by pointing out a way of deducing which is certainly not syllogistic, and does not fit into the mediæval scheme.

The question of the scope and validity of induction is of great difficulty, and of great importance to our knowledge. Take such a question as, " Will the sun rise to-morrow ? " Our first instinctive feeling is that we have abundant reason for saying that it will, because it has risen on so many previous mornings. Now, I do not myself know whether this does afford a ground or not, but I am willing to suppose that it does. The question which then arises is : " What is the principle of inference by which we pass from past sunrises to future ones ? The answer given by Mill is that the inference depends upon the law of causation.

Let us suppose this to be true ; then what is the reason for believing in the law of causation ? There are broadly three possible answers : (1) that it is itself known *a priori* ; (2) that it is a postulate ; (3) that it is an empirical generalization from past instances in which it has been found to hold. The theory that causation is known *a priori* cannot be definitely refuted, but it can be rendered very unplausible by the mere process of formulating the law exactly, and thereby showing that it is immensely more complicated and less obvious than is generally supposed. The theory that causation is a postulate, i.e. that it is something which we choose to assert although we know that it is very likely false, is also incapable of refutation ; but it is plainly also incapable of justifying any use of the law in inference. We are thus brought to the theory that the law is an empirical generalization, which is the view held by Mill.

But if so, how are empirical generalizations to be justified ? The evidence in their favour cannot be empirical, since we wish to argue from what has been observed to what has not been observed, which can only be done by means of some known relation of the observed and the unobserved ; but the unobserved, by definition, is not known empirically, and therefore its relation to the observed, if known at all, must be known independently of empirical evidence. Let us see what Mill says on this subject.

According to Mill, the law of causation is proved by an admittedly fallible process called " induction by simple enumeration." This process, he says, " consists in ascribing the nature of general truths to all propositions which are true in every instance that we happen to know of." [1] As regards its fallibility, he

[1] *Logic*, Book III. chapter iii. § 2.

asserts that "the precariousness of the method of simple enumeration is in an inverse ratio to the largeness of the generalization. The process is delusive and insufficient, exactly in proportion as the subject-matter of the observation is special and limited in extent. As the sphere widens, this unscientific method becomes less and less liable to mislead ; and the most universal class of truths, the law of causation for instance, and the principles of number and of geometry, are duly and satisfactorily proved by that method alone, nor are they susceptible of any other proof." [1]

In the above statement, there are two obvious lacunæ : (1) How is the method of simple enumeration itself justified ? (2) What logical principle, if any, covers the same ground as this method, without being liable to its failures ? Let us take the second question first.

A method of proof which, when used as directed, gives sometimes truth and sometimes falsehood—as the method of simple enumeration does—is obviously not a valid method, for validity demands invariable truth. Thus, if simple enumeration is to be rendered valid, it must not be stated as Mill states it. We shall have to say, at most, that the data render the result *probable*. Causation holds, we shall say, in every instance we have been able to test ; therefore it *probably* holds in untested instances. There are terrible difficulties in the notion of probability, but we may ignore them at present. We thus have what at least *may* be a logical principle, since it is without exception. If a proposition is true in every instance that we happen to know of, and if the instances are very numerous, then, we shall say, it becomes very probable, on the data, that it will be true in any further instance. This

[1] Book III. chapter xxi. § 3.

is not refuted by the fact that what we declare to be probable does not always happen, for an event may be probable on the data and yet not occur. It is, however, obviously capable of further analysis, and of more exact statement. We shall have to say something like this : that every instance of a proposition [1] being true increases the probability of its being true in a fresh instance, and that a sufficient number of favourable instances will, in the absence of instances to the contrary, make the probability of the truth of a fresh instance approach indefinitely near to certainty. Some such principle as this is required if the method of simple enumeration is to be valid.

But this brings us to our other question, namely, how is our principle known to be true ? Obviously, since it is required to justify induction, it cannot be proved by induction ; since it goes beyond the empirical data, it cannot be proved by them alone ; since it is required to justify all inferences from empirical data to what goes beyond them, it cannot itself be even rendered in any degree probable by such data. Hence, *if* it is known, it is not known by experience, but independently of experience. I do not say that any such principle is known : I only say that it is required to justify the inferences from experience which empiricists allow, and that it cannot itself be justified empirically.[2]

A similar conclusion can be proved by similar arguments concerning any other logical principle. Thus logical knowledge is not derivable from experience alone, and the empiricist's philosophy can therefore not be accepted in its entirety, in spite

[1] Or rather a propositional function.
[2] The subject of causality and induction will be discussed again in Lecture VIII.

of its excellence in many matters which lie outside logic.

Hegel and his followers widened the scope of logic in quite a different way—a way which I believe to be fallacious, but which requires discussion if only to show how their conception of logic differs from the conception which I wish to advocate. In their writings, logic is practically identical with metaphysics. In broad outline, the way this came about is as follows. Hegel believed that, by means of *a priori* reasoning, it could be shown that the world *must* have various important and interesting characteristics, since any world without these characteristics would be impossible and self-contradictory. Thus what he calls "logic" is an investigation of the nature of the universe, in so far as this can be inferred merely from the principle that the universe must be logically self-consistent. I do not myself believe that from this principle alone anything of importance can be inferred as regards the existing universe. But, however that may be, I should not regard Hegel's reasoning, even if it were valid, as properly belonging to logic : it would rather be an application of logic to the actual world. Logic itself would be concerned rather with such questions as what self-consistency is, which Hegel, so far as I know, does not discuss. And though he criticizes the traditional logic, and professes to replace it by an improved logic of his own, there is some sense in which the traditional logic, with all its faults, is uncritically and unconsciously assumed throughout his reasoning. It is not in the direction advocated by him, it seems to me, that the reform of logic is to be sought, but by a more fundamental, more patient, and less ambitious investigation into the presuppositions which his system shares with those of most other philosophers.

The way in which, as it seems to me, Hegel's system assumes the ordinary logic which it subsequently criticizes, is exemplified by the general conception of " categories " with which he operates throughout. This conception is, I think, essentially a product of logical confusion, but it seems in some way to stand for the conception of " qualities of Reality as a whole." Mr. Bradley has worked out a theory according to which, in all judgment, we are ascribing a predicate to Reality as a whole ; and this theory is derived from Hegel. Now the traditional logic holds that every proposition ascribes a predicate to a subject, and from this it easily follows that there can be only one subject, the Absolute, for if there were two, the proposition that there were two would not ascribe a predicate to either. Thus Hegel's doctrine, that philosophical propositions must be of the form, " the Absolute is such-and-such," depends upon the traditional belief in the universality of the subject-predicate form. This belief, being traditional, scarcely self-conscious, and not supposed to be important, operates underground, and is assumed in arguments which, like the refutation of relations, appear at first sight such as to establish its truth. This is the most important respect in which Hegel uncritically assumes the traditional logic. Other less important respects—though important enough to be the source of such essentially Hegelian conceptions as the " concrete universal " and the " union of identity in difference "—will be found where he explicitly deals with formal logic.[1]

---

[1] See the translation by H. S. Macran, *Hegel's Doctrine of Formal Logic*, Oxford, 1912. Hegel's argument in this portion of his " Logic " depends throughout upon confusing the " is " of predication, as in " Socrates is mortal," with the " is " of identity, as in " Socrates is the philosopher who drank

There is quite another direction in which a large technical development of logic has taken place : I mean the direction of what is called logistic or mathematical logic This kind of logic is mathematical in two different senses : it is itself a branch of mathematics, and it is the logic which is specially applicable to other more traditional branches of mathematics. Historically, it began as *merely* a branch of mathematics: its special applicability to other branches is a more recent development. In both respects, it is the fulfilment of a hope which Leibniz cherished throughout his life, and pursued with all the ardour of his amazing intellectual energy. Much of his work on this subject has been published recently, since his discoveries have been remade by others ; but none was published by him, because his results persisted in contradicting certain points in the traditional doctrine of the syllogism. We now know that on these points the traditional doctrine is wrong, but respect for Aristotle prevented Leibniz from realizing that this was possible.[1]

The modern development of mathematical logic

the hemlock." Owing to this confusion, he thinks that " Socrates " and " mortal " must be identical. Seeing that they are different, he does not infer, as others would, that there is a mistake somewhere, but that they exhibit " identity in difference." Again, Socrates is particular, " mortal " is universal. Therefore, he says, since Socrates is mortal, it follows that the particular is the universal—taking the " is " to be throughout expressive of identity. But to say " the particular is the universal " is self-contradictory. Again Hegel does not suspect a mistake but proceeds to synthesize particular and universal in the individual, or concrete universal. This is an example of how, for want of care at the start, vast and imposing systems of philosophy are built upon stupid and trivial confusions, which, but for the almost incredible fact that they are unintentional, one would be tempted to characterize as puns.

[1] Cf. Couturat, *La Logique de Leibniz*, pp. 361, 386.

dates from Boole's *Laws of Thought* (1854). But in him and his successors, before Peano and Frege, the only thing really achieved, apart from certain details, was the invention of a mathematical symbolism for deducing consequences from the premisses which the newer methods shared with those of Aristotle. This subject has considerable interest as an independent branch of mathematics, but it has very little to do with real logic. The first serious advance in real logic since the time of the Greeks was made independently by Peano and Frege—both mathematicians. They both arrived at their logical results by an analysis of mathematics. Traditional logic regarded the two propositions, " Socrates is mortal " and " All men are mortal," as being of the same form ; [1] Peano and Frege showed that they are utterly different in form. The philosophical importance of logic may be illustrated by the fact that this confusion—which is still committed by most writers—obscured not only the whole study of the forms of judgment and inference, but also the relations of things to their qualities, of concrete existence to abstract concepts, and of the world of sense to the world of Platonic ideas. Peano and Frege, who pointed out the error, did so for technical reasons, and applied their logic mainly to technical developments ; but the philosophical importance of the advance which they made is impossible to exaggerate.

Mathematical logic, even in its most modern form, is not *directly* of philosophical importance except in its beginnings. After the beginnings, it belongs rather to mathematics than to philosophy. Of its beginnings, which are the only part of it that can

---

[1] It was often recognized that there was *some* difference between them, but it was not recognized that the difference is fundamental, and of very great importance.

properly be called *philosophical* logic, I shall speak
shortly. But even the later developments, though
not directly philosophical, will be found of great indirect
use in philosophizing. They enable us to deal easily
with more abstract conceptions than merely verbal
reasoning can enumerate ; they suggest fruitful hypotheses which otherwise could hardly be thought of ;
and they enable us to see quickly what is the smallest
store of materials with which a given logical or scientific
edifice can be constructed. Not only Frege's theory
of number, which we shall deal with in Lecture VII,
but the whole theory of physical concepts which will
be outlined in our next two lectures, is inspired by
mathematical logic, and could never have been
imagined without it.

In both these cases, and in many others, we shall
appeal to a certain principle called " the principle of
abstraction." This principle, which might equally well
be called " the principle which dispenses with abstraction," and is one which clears away incredible accumu-
lations of metaphysical lumber, was directly suggested
by mathematical logic, and could hardly have been
proved or practically used without its help. The
principle will be explained in our fourth lecture, but
its use may be briefly indicated in advance. When a
group of objects have that kind of similarity which
we are inclined to attribute to possession of a common
quality, the principle in question shows that membership
of the group will serve all the purposes of the supposed
common quality, and that therefore, unless some
common quality is actually known, the group or class
of similar objects may be used to replace the common
quality, which need not be assumed to exist. In this
and other ways, the indirect uses of even the later parts
of mathematical logic are very great ; but it is now

time to turn our attention to its philosophical foundations.

In every proposition and in every inference there is, besides the particular subject-matter concerned, a certain *form*, a way in which the constituents of the proposition or inference are put together. If I say, " Socrates is mortal," " Jones is angry," " The sun is hot," there is something in common in these three cases, something indicated by the word " is." What is in common is the *form* of the proposition, not an actual constituent. If I say a number of things about Socrates—that he was an Athenian, that he married Xantippe, that he drank the hemlock—there is a common constituent, namely Socrates, in all the propositions I enunciate, but they have diverse forms. If, on the other hand, I take any one of these propositions and replace its constituents, one at a time, by other constituents, the form remains constant, but no constituent remains. Take (say) the series of propositions, " Socrates drank the hemlock," " Coleridge drank the hemlock," " Coleridge drank opium," " Coleridge ate opium." The form remains unchanged throughout this series, but all the constituents are altered. Thus form is not another constituent, but is the way the constituents are put together. It is forms, in this sense, that are the proper object of philosophical logic.

It is obvious that the knowledge of logical forms is something quite different from knowledge of existing things. The form of " Socrates drank the hemlock " is not an existing thing like Socrates or the hemlock, nor does it even have that close relation to existing things that drinking has. It is something altogether more abstract and remote. We might understand all the separate words of a sentence without understanding the sentence : if a sentence is long and complicated, this is apt to happen. In such a case we have knowledge of the constituents, but not of the form. We may also have knowledge of the form without having knowledge of the constituents. If I say, " Rorarius drank the hemlock," those among you who have never heard of Rorarius (supposing there are any) will understand the form, without having knowledge of all the constituents. In order to understand a sentence, it is necessary to have knowledge both of the constituents and of the particular instance of the form. It is in this way that a sentence conveys information, since it tells us that certain known objects are related according to a certain known form. Thus some kind of knowledge of logical forms, though with most people it is not explicit, is involved in all understanding of discourse. It is the business of philosophical logic to extract this knowledge from its concrete integuments, and to render it explicit and pure.

In all inference, form alone is essential : the particular subject-matter is irrelevant except as securing the truth of the premisses. This is one reason for the great importance of logical form. When I say, "Socrates was a man, all men are mortal, therefore Socrates was mortal," the connection of premisses and conclusion does not in any way depend upon its being Socrates and man and mortality that I am mentioning. The general form of the inference may be expressed in some such words as: " If a thing has a certain property, and whatever has this property has a certain other property, then the thing in question also has that other property." Here no particular things or properties are mentioned : the proposition is absolutely general. All inferences, when stated fully, are instances of propositions having this kind of generality. If they seem to depend upon the subject-matter otherwise than as regards the truth of the premisses, that is because the premisses have not been all explicitly stated. In logic, it is a waste of time to deal with inferences concerning particular cases : we deal throughout with completely general and purely formal implications, leaving it to other sciences to discover when the hypotheses are verified and when they are not.

But the forms of propositions giving rise to inferences are not the simplest forms ; they are always hypothetical, stating that if one proposition is true, then so is another. Before considering inference, therefore, logic must consider those simpler forms which inference presupposes. Here the traditional logic failed completely : it believed that there was only one form of simple proposition (i.e. of proposition not stating a relation between two or more other propositions), namely, the form which ascribes a predicate to a subject. This is the appropriate form in assigning the qualities of a given thing—we may say " this thing is round, and red, and so on." Grammar favours this form, but philosophically it is so far from universal that it is not even very common. If we say " this thing is bigger than that," we are not assigning a mere quality of " this," but a relation of " this " and " that." We might express the same fact by saying " that thing is smaller than this," where grammatically the subject is changed. Thus propositions stating that two things have a certain relation have a different form from subject-predicate propositions, and the failure to perceive this difference or to allow for it has been the source of many errors in traditional metaphysics.

The belief or unconscious conviction that all propo-

sitions are of the subject-predicate form—in other
words: that every fact consists in some thing having
some quality—has rendered most philosophers incapable
of giving any account of the world of science and daily
life. If they had been honestly anxious to give such
an account, they would probably have discovered
their error very quickly ; but most of them were less
anxious to understand the world of science and daily
life, than to convict it of unreality in the interests
of a super-sensible "real" world. Belief in the
unreality of the world of sense arises with irresistible
force in certain moods—moods which, I imagine, have
some simple physiological basis, but are none the
less powerfully persuasive. The conviction born of
these moods is the source of most mysticism and
of most metaphysics. When the emotional intensity of
such a mood subsides, a man who is in the habit of
reasoning will search for logical reasons in favour
of the belief which he finds in himself. But since the
belief already exists, he will be very hospitable to any
reason that suggests itself. The paradoxes apparently
proved by his logic are really the paradoxes of mysticism,
and are the goal which he feels his logic must reach
if it is to be in accordance with insight. It is in this
way that logic has been pursued by those of the great
philosophers who were mystics—notably Plato, Spinoza,
and Hegel. But since they usually took for granted
the supposed insight of the mystic emotion, their
logical doctrines were presented with a certain dryness,
and were believed by their disciples to be quite independent of the sudden illumination from which they
sprang. Nevertheless their origin clung to them, and
they remained—to borrow a useful word from Mr.
Santayana—" malicious " in regard to the world of
science and common sense. It is only so that we

can account for the complacency with which philosophers have accepted the inconsistence of their doctrines with all the common and scientific facts which seem best established and most worthy of belief.

The logic of mysticism shows, as is natural, the defects which are inherent in anything malicious. While the mystic mood is dominant, the need of logic is not felt ; as the mood fades, the impulse to logic reasserts itself, but with a desire to retain the vanishing insight, or at least to prove that it *was* insight, and that what seems to contradict it is illusion. The logic which thus arises is not quite disinterested or candid, and is inspired by a certain hatred of the daily world to which it is to be applied. Such an attitude naturally does not tend to the best results. Everyone knows that to read an author simply in order to refute him is not the way to understand him ; and to read the book of Nature with a conviction that it is all illusion is just as unlikely to lead to understanding. If our logic is to find the common world intelligible, it must not be hostile, but must be inspired by a genuine acceptance such as is not usually to be found among metaphysicians.

Traditional logic, since it holds that all propositions have the subject-predicate form, is unable to admit the reality of relations : all relations, it maintains, must be reduced to properties of the apparently related terms. There are many ways of refuting this opinion ; one of the easiest is derived from the consideration of what are called " asymmetrical " relations. In order to explain this, I will first explain two independent ways of classifying relations.

Some relations, when they hold between A and B, also hold between B and A. Such, for example, is the relation " brother or sister." If A is a brother or

sister of B then B is a brother or sister of A. Such
again is any kind of similarity, say similarity of colour.
Any kind of dissimilarity is also of this kind : if the
colour of A is unlike the colour of B, then the colour of
B is unlike the colour of A. Relations of this sort are
called *symmetrical*. Thus a relation is symmetrical
if, whenever it holds between A and B, it also holds
between B and A.

All relations that are not symmetrical are called
non-symmetrical. Thus " brother " is non-symmetrical,
because, if A is a brother of B, it may happen that
B is a *sister* of A.

A relation is called *asymmetrical* when, if it holds
between A and B, it *never* holds between B and A.
Thus husband, father, grandfather, etc., are asymmetrical relations. So are *before, after, greater, above,
to the right of*, etc. All the relations that give rise to
series are of this kind.

Classification into symmetrical, asymmetrical and
merely non-symmetrical relations is the first of the
two classifications we had to consider. The second
is into transitive, intransitive, and merely non-transitive
relations, which are defined as follows.

A relation is said to be *transitive*, if, whenever it
holds between A and B and also between B and C,
it holds between A and C. Thus *before, after, greater,
above* are transitive. All relations giving rise to series
are transitive, but so are many others. The transitive
relations just mentioned were asymmetrical, but
many transitive relations are symmetrical—for instance,
equality in any respect, exact identity of colour, being
equally numerous (as applied to collections), and
so on.

A relation is said to be *non-transitive* whenever it
is not transitive. Thus " brother " is non-transitive,

because a brother of one's brother may be oneself. All kinds of dissimilarity are non-transitive.

A relation is said to be *intransitive* when, if A has the relation to B, and B to C, A never has it to C. Thus "father" is intransitive. So is such a relation as "one inch taller" or "one year later."

Let us now, in the light of this classification, return to the question whether all relations can be reduced to predications.

In the case of symmetrical relations—i.e. relations which, if they hold between A and B, also hold between B and A—some kind of plausibility can be given to this doctrine. A symmetrical relation which is transitive, such as equality, can be regarded as expressing possession of some common property, while one which is not transitive, such as inequality, can be regarded as expressing possession of different properties. But when we come to asymmetrical relations, such as before and after, greater and less, etc., the attempt to reduce them to properties becomes obviously impossible. When, for example, two things are merely known to be unequal, without our knowing which is greater, we may say that the inequality results from their having different magnitudes, because inequality is a symmetrical relation; but to say that when one thing is *greater* than another, and not merely unequal to it, that means that they have different magnitudes, is formally incapable of explaining the facts. For if the other thing had been greater than the one, the magnitudes would also have been different, though the fact to be explained would not have been the same. Thus mere *difference* of magnitude is not *all* that is involved, since, if it were, there would be no difference between one thing being greater than another, and the other being greater than the one. We shall have to say that the one magnitude is *greater* than the *other*, and thus we shall have failed to get rid of the relation " greater." In short, both possession of the same property and possession of different properties are *symmetrical* relations, and therefore cannot account for the existence of *asymmetrical* relations.

Asymmetrical relations are involved in all series— in space and time, greater and less, whole and part, and many others of the most important characteristics of the actual world. All these aspects, therefore, the logic which reduces everything to subjects and predicates is compelled to condemn as error and mere appearance. To those whose logic is not malicious, such a wholesale condemnation appears impossible. And in fact there is no reason except prejudice, so far as I can discover, for denying the reality of relations. When once their reality is admitted, all *logical* grounds for supposing the world of sense to be illusory disappear. If this is to be supposed, it must be frankly and simply on the ground of mystic insight unsupported by argument. It is impossible to argue against what professes to be insight, so long as it does not argue in its own favour. As logicians, therefore, we may admit the possibility of the mystic's world, while yet, so long as we do not have his insight, we must continue to study the everyday world with which we are familiar. But when he contends that our world is impossible, then our logic is ready to repel his attack. And the first step in creating the logic which is to perform this service is the recognition of the reality of relations.

Relations which have two terms are only one kind of relations. A relation may have three terms, or four, or any number. Relations of two terms, being the simplest, have received more attention than the others, and have generally been alone considered by philosophers, both those who accepted and those who denied the reality of relations. But other relations have their importance, and are indispensable in the solution of certain problems. Jealousy, for example, is a relation between three people. Professor Royce mentions the relation " giving " : when A gives B to C, that is a relation of three terms.[1] When a man says to his wife : " My dear, I wish you could induce Angelina to accept Edwin," his wish constitutes a relation between four people, himself, his wife, Angelina, and Edwin. Thus such relations are by no means recondite or rare. But in order to explain exactly how they differ from relations of two terms, we must embark upon a classification of the logical forms of facts, which is the first business of logic, and the business in which the traditional logic has been most deficient.

The existing world consists of many things with many qualities and relations. A complete description of the existing world would require not only a catalogue of the things, but also a mention of all their qualities and relations. We should have to know not only this that, and the other thing, but also which was red, which yellow, which was earlier than which, which was which between two others, and so on. When I speak of a " fact," I do not mean one of the simple things in the world ; I mean that a certain thing has a certain quality, or that certain things have a certain relation. Thus, for example, I should not call Napoleon a fact, but I should call it a fact that he was ambitious, or that he married Josephine. Now a fact, in this sense, is never simple, but always has two or more constituents. When it simply assigns a quality to a thing,

[1] *Encyclopædia of the Philosophical Sciences*, vol. i. p. 97.

it has only two constituents, the thing and the quality. When it consists of a relation between two things, it has three constituents, the things and the relation. When it consists of a relation between three things, it has four constituents, and so on. The constituents of facts, in the sense in which we are using the word " fact," are not other facts, but are things and qualities or relations. When we say that there are relations of more than two terms, we mean that there are single facts consisting of a single relation and more than two things. I do not mean that one relation of two terms may hold between A and B, and also between A and C, as, for example, a man is the son of his father and also the son of his mother. This constitutes two distinct facts : if we choose to treat it as one fact, it is a fact which has facts for its constituents. But the facts I am speaking of have no facts among their constituents, but only things and relations. For example, when A is jealous of B on account of C, there is only one fact, involving three people ; there are not two instances of jealousy, but only one. It is in such cases that I speak of a relation of three terms, where the simplest possible fact in which the relation occurs is one involving three things in addition to the relation. And the same applies to relations of four terms or five or any other number. All such relations must be admitted in our inventory of the logical forms of facts : two facts involving the same number of things have the same form, and two which involve different numbers of things have different forms.

Given any fact, there is an assertion which expresses the fact. The fact itself is objective, and independent of our thought or opinion about it ; but the assertion is something which involves thought, and may be either true or false. An assertion may be positive or negative : we may assert that Charles I was executed, or that he did *not* die in his bed. A negative assertion may be said to be a *denial*. Given a form of words which must be either true or false, such as " Charles I died in his bed," we may either assert or deny this form of words : in the one case we have a positive assertion, in the other a negative one. A form of words which must be either true or false I shall call a *proposition*. Thus a proposition is the same as what may be significantly asserted or denied. A proposition which expresses what we have called a fact, i.e. which, when asserted, asserts that a certain thing has a certain quality, or that certain things have a certain relation, will be called an atomic proposition, because, as we shall see immediately, there are other propositions into which atomic propositions enter in a way analogous to that in which atoms enter into molecules. Atomic propositions, although, like facts, they may have any one of an infinite number of forms, are only one kind of propositions. All other kinds are more complicated. In order to preserve the parallelism in language as regards facts and propositions, we shall give the name " atomic facts " to the facts we have hitherto been considering. Thus atomic facts are what determine whether atomic propositions are to be asserted or denied.

Whether an atomic proposition, such as " this is red," or " this is before that," is to be asserted or denied can only be known empirically. Perhaps one atomic fact may sometimes be capable of being inferred from another, though this seems very doubtful ; but in any case it cannot be inferred from premises no one of which is an atomic fact. It follows that, if atomic facts are to be known at all, some at least must be known without inference. The atomic facts which we come to know in this way are the facts of sense-perception ; at any rate, the facts of sense-perception are those which we most obviously and certainly come to know in this way. If we knew all atomic facts, and also knew that there were none except those we knew, we should, theoretically, be able to infer all truths of whatever form.[1] Thus logic would then supply us with the whole of the apparatus required. But in the first acquisition of knowledge concerning atomic facts, logic is useless. In pure logic, no atomic fact is ever mentioned : we confine ourselves wholly to forms, without asking ourselves what objects can fill the forms. Thus pure logic is independent of atomic facts ; but conversely, they are, in a sense, independent of logic. Pure logic and atomic facts are the two poles, the wholly *a priori* and the wholly empirical. But between the two lies a vast intermediate region, which we must now briefly explore.

" Molecular " propositions are such as contain conjunctions—*if, or, and, unless*, etc.—and such words are the marks of a molecular proposition. Consider such an assertion as, " If it rains, I shall bring my umbrella." This assertion is just as capable of truth or falsehood as the assertion of an atomic proposition, but it is obvious that either the corresponding fact, or the nature of the correspondence with fact, must be quite different from what it is in the case of an atomic proposition. Whether it rains, and whether I bring my umbrella, are each severally matters of atomic

[1] This perhaps requires modification in order to include such facts as beliefs and wishes, since such facts apparently contain propositions as components. Such facts, though not strictly atomic, must be supposed included if the statement in the text is to be true.

fact, ascertainable by observation. But the connection of the two involved in saying that *if* the one happens, *then* the other will happen, is something radically different from either of the two separately. It does not require for its truth that it should actually rain, or that I should actually bring my umbrella ; even if the weather is cloudless, it may still be true that I should have brought my umbrella if the weather had been different. Thus we have here a connection of two propositions, which does not depend upon whether they are to be asserted or denied, but only upon the second being inferable from the first. Such propositions, therefore, have a form which is different from that of any atomic proposition.

Such propositions are important to logic, because all inference depends upon them. If I have told you that if it rains I shall bring my umbrella, and if you see that there is a steady downpour, you can infer that I shall bring my umbrella. There can be no inference except where propositions are connected in some such way, so that from the truth or falsehood of the one something follows as to the truth or falsehood of the other. It seems to be the case that we can sometimes know molecular propositions, as in the above instance of the umbrella, when we do not know whether the component atomic propositions are true or false. The *practical* utility of inference rests upon this fact.

The next kind of propositions we have to consider are *general* propositions, such as " all men are mortal," " all equilateral triangles are equiangular." And with these belong propositions in which the word " some " occurs, such as " some men are philosophers " or " some philosophers are not wise." These are the denials of general propositions, namely (in the above instances), of " all men are non-philosophers " and " all philosophers are wise." We will call propositions containing the word " some " *negative* general propositions, and those containing the word " all " *positive* general propositions. These propositions, it will be seen, begin to have the appearance of the propositions in logical text-books. But their peculiarity and complexity are not known to the text-books, and the problems which they raise are only discussed in the most superficial manner.

When we were discussing atomic facts, we saw that we should be able, theoretically, to infer all other truths by logic if we knew all atomic facts and also knew that there were no other atomic facts besides those we knew. The knowledge that there are no other atomic facts is positive general knowledge ; it is the knowledge that " all atomic facts are known to me," or at least " all atomic facts are in this collection "—however the collection may be given. It is easy to see that general propositions, such as " all men are mortal," cannot be known by inference from atomic facts alone. If we could know each individual man, and know that he was mortal, that would not enable us to know that all men are mortal, unless we *knew* that those were all the men there are, which is a general proposition. If we knew every other existing thing throughout the universe, and knew that each separate thing was not an immortal man, that would not give us our result unless we *knew* that we had explored the whole universe, i.e. unless we knew " all things belong to this collection of things I have examined." Thus general truths cannot be inferred from particular truths alone, but must, if they are to be known, be either self-evident or inferred from premisses of which at least one is a general truth. But all *empirical* evidence is of *particular* truths. Hence, if there is any knowledge of general truths at all, there must be *some* knowledge of general truths which is independent of empirical evidence, i.e. does not depend upon the data of sense.

The above conclusion, of which we had an instance in the case of the inductive principle, is important, since it affords a refutation of the older empiricists. They believed that all our knowledge is derived from the senses and dependent upon them. We see that, if this view is to be maintained, we must refuse to admit that we know any general propositions. It is perfectly possible logically that this should be the case, but it does not appear to be so in fact, and indeed no one would dream of maintaining such a view except a theorist at the last extremity. We must therefore admit that there is general knowledge not derived from sense, and that some of this knowledge is not obtained by inference but is primitive.

Such general knowledge is to be found in logic. Whether there is any such knowledge not derived from logic, I do not know ; but in logic, at any rate, we have such knowledge. It will be remembered that we excluded from pure logic such propositions as, " Socrates is a man, all men are mortal, therefore Socrates is mortal," because Socrates and *man* and *mortal* are empirical terms, only to be understood through particular experience. The corresponding proposition in pure logic is : " If anything has a certain property, and whatever has this property has a certain other property, then the thing in question has the other property." This proposition is absolutely general : it applies to all things and all properties. And it is quite self-evident. Thus in such propositions of pure logic we have the self-evident general propositions of which we were in search.

A proposition such as " If Socrates is a man, and all men are mortal, then Socrates is mortal," is true in virtue of its *form* alone. Its truth, in this hypothetical form, does not depend upon whether Socrates actually is a man, nor upon whether in fact all men are mortal ; thus it is equally true when we substitute other terms for Socrates and *man* and *mortal*. The general truth of which it is an instance is purely formal, and belongs to logic. Since this general truth does not mention any particular thing, or even any particular quality or relation, it is wholly independent of the accidental facts of the existent world, and can be known, theoretically, without any experience of particular things or their qualities and relations.

Logic, we may say, consists of two parts. The first part investigates what propositions are and what forms they may have ; this part enumerates the different kinds of atomic propositions, of molecular propositions, of general propositions, and so on. The second part consists of certain supremely general propositions, which assert the truth of all propositions of certain forms. This second part merges into pure mathematics, whose propositions all turn out, on analysis, to be such general formal truths. The first part, which merely enumerates forms, is the more difficult, and philosophically the more important ; and it is the recent progress in this first part, more than anything else, that has rendered a truly scientific discussion of many philosophical problems possible.

The problem of the nature of judgment or belief may be taken as an example of a problem whose solution depends upon an adequate inventory of logical forms. We have already seen how the supposed universality of the subject-predicate form made it impossible to give a right analysis of serial order, and therefore made space and time unintelligible. But in this case it was only necessary to admit relations of two terms. The case of judgment demands the admission of more complicated forms. If all judgments were true, we might suppose that a judgment consisted in apprehension of a *fact*, and that the apprehension was a relation of a mind to the fact. From poverty in the logical inventory, this view has often been held. But it leads to absolutely insoluble difficulties in the case of error. Suppose I believe that Charles I died in his bed. There is no objective fact " Charles I's death in his bed " to which I can have a relation of apprehension. Charles I and death and his bed are objective, but they are not, except in my thought, put together as my false belief supposes. It is therefore necessary, in analysing a belief, to look for some other logical form than a two-term relation. Failure to realize this necessity has, in my opinion, vitiated almost everything that has hitherto been written on the theory of knowledge, making the problem of error insoluble and the difference between belief and perception inexplicable.

Modern logic, as I hope is now evident, has the effect of enlarging our abstract imagination, and providing an infinite number of possible hypotheses to be applied in the analysis of any complex fact. In this respect it is the exact opposite of the logic practised by the classical tradition. In that logic, hypotheses which seem *prima facie* possible are professedly proved impossible, and it is decreed in advance that reality must have a certain special character. In modern logic, on the contrary, while the *prima facie* hypotheses as a rule remain admissible, others, which only logic would have suggested, are added to our stock, and are very often found to be indispensable if a right analysis of the facts is to be obtained. The old logic put thought in fetters, while the new logic gives it wings. It has, in my opinion, introduced the same kind of advance into philosophy as Galileo introduced into physics, making it possible at last to see what kinds of problems may be capable of solution, and what kinds must be abandoned as beyond human powers. And where a solution appears possible, the new logic provides a method which enables us to obtain results that do not merely embody personal idiosyncrasies, but must command the assent of all who are competent to form an opinion.

LECTURE III

ON OUR KNOWLEDGE OF THE EXTERNAL WORLD

PHILOSOPHY may be approached by many roads, but one of the oldest and most travelled is the road which leads through doubt as to the reality of the world of sense. In Indian mysticism, in Greek and modern monistic philosophy from Parmenides onward, in Berkeley, in modern physics, we find sensible appearance criticized and condemned for a bewildering variety of motives. The mystic condemns it on the ground of immediate knowledge of a more real and significant world behind the veil; Parmenides and Plato condemn it because its continual flux is thought inconsistent with the unchanging nature of the abstract entities revealed by logical analysis; Berkeley brings several weapons, but his chief is the subjectivity of sense-data, their dependence upon the organization and point of view of the spectator; while modern physics, on the basis of sensible evidence itself, maintains a mad dance of electrons which have, superficially at least, very little resemblance to the immediate objects of sight or touch.

Every one of these lines of attack raises vital and interesting problems.

The mystic, so long as he merely reports a positive revelation, cannot be refuted; but when he *denies* reality to objects of sense, he may be questioned as to what he means by " reality," and may be asked how their unreality follows from the supposed reality of his super-sensible world. In answering these questions, he is led to a logic which merges into that of Parmenides and Plato and the idealist tradition.

The logic of the idealist tradition has gradually grown very complex and very abstruse, as may be seen from the Bradleian sample considered in our first lecture. If we attempted to deal fully with this logic, we should not have time to reach any other aspect of our subject ; we will therefore, while acknowledging that it deserves a long discussion, pass by its central doctrines with only such occasional criticism as may serve to exemplify other topics, and concentrate our attention on such matters as its objections to the continuity of motion and the infinity of space and time—objections which have been fully answered by modern mathematicians in a manner constituting an abiding triumph for the method of logical analysis in philosophy. These objections and the modern answers to them will occupy our fifth, sixth, and seventh lectures.

Berkeley's attack, as reinforced by the physiology of the sense-organs and nerves and brain, is very powerful. I think it must be admitted as probable that the immediate objects of sense depend for their existence upon physiological conditions in ourselves, and that, for example, the coloured surfaces which we see cease to exist when we shut our eyes. But it would be a mistake to infer that they are dependent upon mind, not real while we see them, or not the sole basis for our knowledge of the external world. This line of argument will be developed in the present lecture.

The discrepancy between the world of physics and the world of sense, which we shall consider in our fourth lecture, will be found to be more apparent than real, and it will be shown that whatever there is reason to believe in physics can probably be interpreted consistently with the reality of sense-data.

The instrument of discovery throughout is modern logic, a very different science from the logic of the text-books and also from the logic of idealism. Our second lecture has given a short account of modern logic and of its points of divergence from the various traditional kinds of logic.

In our last lecture, after a discussion of causality and free will, we shall try to reach a general account of the logical-analytic method of scientific philosophy, and a tentative estimate of the hopes of philosophical progress which it allows us to entertain.

In this lecture, I wish to apply the logical-analytic method to one of the oldest problems of philosophy, namely, the problem of our knowledge of the external world. What I have to say on this problem does not amount to an answer of a definite and dogmatic kind ; it amounts only to an analysis and statement of the questions involved, with an indication of the directions in which evidence may be sought. But although not yet a definite solution, what can be said at present seems to me to throw a completely new light on the problem, and to be indispensable, not only in seeking the answer, but also in the preliminary question as to what parts of our problem may possibly have an ascertainable answer.

In every philosophical problem, our investigation starts from what may be called " data," by which I mean matters of common knowledge, vague, complex, inexact, as common knowledge always is, but yet somehow commanding our assent as on the whole and in some interpretation pretty certainly true. In the case of our present problem, the common knowledge involved is of various kinds. There is first our acquaintance with particular objects of daily life—furniture, houses, towns, other people, and so on. Then there is the extension of such particular knowledge to particular things outside our personal experience, through history and geography, newspapers, etc. And lastly, there is the systematization of all this knowledge of particulars by means of physical science, which derives immense persuasive force from its astonishing power of foretelling the future. We are quite willing to admit that there may be errors of detail in this knowledge, but we believe them to be discoverable and corrigible by the methods which have given rise to our beliefs, and we do not, as practical men, entertain for a moment the hypothesis that the whole edifice may be built on insecure foundations. In the main, therefore, and without absolute dogmatism as to this or that special portion, we may accept this mass of common knowledge as affording data for our philosophical analysis.

It may be said—and this is an objection which must be met at the outset—that it is the duty of the philosopher to call in question the admittedly fallible beliefs of daily life, and to replace them by something more solid and irrefragable. In a sense this is true, and in a sense it is effected in the course of analysis. But in another sense, and a very important one, it is quite impossible. While admitting that doubt is possible with regard to all our common knowledge, we must nevertheless accept that knowledge in the main if philosophy is to be possible at all. There is not any superfine brand of knowledge, obtainable by the philosopher, which can give us a standpoint from which to criticize the whole of the knowledge of daily life.

The most that can be done is to examine and purify our common knowledge by an internal scrutiny, assuming the canons by which it has been obtained, and applying them with more care and with more precision. Philosophy cannot boast of having achieved such a degree of certainty that it can have authority to condemn the facts of experience and the laws of science. The philosophic scrutiny, therefore, though sceptical in regard to every detail, is not sceptical as regards the whole. That is to say, its criticism of details will only be based upon their relation to other details, not upon some external criterion which can be applied to all the details equally. The reason for this abstention from a universal criticism is not any dogmatic confidence, but its exact opposite ; it is not that common knowledge *must* be true, but that we possess no radically different kind of knowledge derived from some other source. Universal scepticism, though logically irrefutable, is practically barren ; it can only, therefore, give a certain flavour of hesitancy to our beliefs, and cannot be used to substitute other beliefs for them.

Although data can only be criticized by other data, not by an outside standard, yet we may distinguish different grades of certainty in the different kinds of common knowledge which we enumerated just now. What does not go beyond our own personal sensible acquaintance must be for us the most certain : the " evidence of the senses " is proverbially the least open to question. What depends on testimony, like the facts of history and geography which are learnt from books, has varying degrees of certainty according to the nature and extent of the testimony. Doubts as to the existence of Napoleon can only be maintained for a joke, whereas the historicity of Agamemnon is

a legitimate subject of debate.   In science, again, we
find all grades of certainty short of the highest.   The
law of gravitation, at least as an approximate truth,
has acquired by this time the same kind of certainty
as the existence of Napoleon, whereas the latest speculations concerning the constitution of matter would
be universally acknowledged to have as yet only a
rather slight probability in their favour.   These varying
degrees of certainty attaching to different data may
be regarded as themselves forming part of our data ;
they, along with the other data, lie within the vague,
complex, inexact body of knowledge which it is the
business of the philosopher to analyse.

The first thing that appears when we begin to analyse
our common knowledge is that some of it is derivative,
while some is primitive ; that is to say, there is some
that we only believe because of something else from
which it has been inferred in some sense, though not
necessarily in a strict logical sense, while other parts
are believed on their own account, without the support
of any outside evidence.   It is obvious that the senses
give knowledge of the latter kind : the immediate
facts perceived by sight or touch or hearing do not
need to be proved by argument, but are completely
self-evident.   Psychologists, however, have made us
aware that what is actually given in sense is much
less than most people would naturally suppose, and
that much of what at first sight seems to be given is
really inferred.   This applies especially in regard to our
space-perceptions.   For instance, we unconsciously infer
the " real " size and shape of a visible object from its
apparent size and shape, according to its distance and
our point of view.   When we hear a person speaking,
our actual sensations usually miss a great deal of what
he says, and we supply its place by unconscious

inference ; in a foreign language, where this process is more difficult, we find ourselves apparently grown deaf, requiring, for example, to be much nearer the stage at a theatre than would be necessary in our own country. Thus the first step in the analysis of data, namely, the discovery of what is really given in sense, is full of difficulty. We will, however, not linger on this point ; so long as its existence is realized, the exact outcome does not make any very great difference in our main problem.

The next step in our analysis must be the consideration of how the derivative parts of our common knowledge arise. Here we become involved in a somewhat puzzling entanglement of logic and psychology. Psychologically, a belief may be called derivative whenever it is caused by one or more other beliefs, or by some fact of sense which is not simply what the belief asserts. Derivative beliefs in this sense constantly arise without any process of logical inference, merely by association of ideas or some equally extralogical process. From the expression of a man's face we judge as to what he is feeling : we say we *see* that he is angry, when in fact we only see a frown. We do not judge as to his state of mind by any logical process : the judgment grows up, often without our being able to say what physical mark of emotion we actually saw. In such a case, the knowledge is derivative psychologically ; but logically it is in a sense primitive, since it is not the result of any logical deduction. There may or may not be a possible deduction leading to the same result, but whether there is or not, we certainly do not employ it. If we call a belief " logically primitive " when it is not actually arrived at by a logical inference, then innumerable beliefs are logically primitive which psychologically are derivative. The separation of these two kinds of primitiveness is vitally important to our present discussion.

When we reflect upon the beliefs which are logically but not psychologically primitive, we find that, unless they can on reflection be deduced by a logical process from beliefs which are also psychologically primitive, our confidence in their truth tends to diminish the more we think about them. We naturally believe, for example, that tables and chairs, trees and mountains, are still there when we turn our backs upon them. I do not wish for a moment to maintain that this is certainly not the case, but I do maintain that the question whether it is the case is not to be settled off-hand on any supposed ground of obviousness. The belief that they persist is, in all men except a few philosophers, logically primitive, but it is not psychologically primitive ; psychologically, it arises only through our having seen those tables and chairs, trees and mountains. As soon as the question is seriously raised whether, because we have seen them, we have a right to suppose that they are there still, we feel that some kind of argument must be produced, and that if none is forthcoming, our belief can be no more than a pious opinion. We do not feel this as regards the immediate objects of sense : there they are, and as far as their momentary existence is concerned, no further argument is required. There is accordingly more need of justifying our psychologically derivative beliefs than of justifying those that are primitive.

We are thus led to a somewhat vague distinction between what we may call " hard " data and " soft " data. This distinction is a matter of degree, and must not be pressed ; but if not taken too seriously, it may help to make the situation clear. I mean by " hard " data those which resist the solvent influence of critical reflection, and by " soft " data those which, under the operation of this process, become to our minds more or less doubtful. The hardest of hard data are of two sorts : the particular facts of sense, and the general truths of logic. The more we reflect upon these, the more we realize exactly what they are, and exactly what a doubt concerning them really means, the more luminously certain do they become. *Verbal* doubt concerning even these is possible, but verbal doubt may occur when what is nominally being doubted is not really in our thoughts, and only words are actually present to our minds. Real doubt, in these two cases, would, I think, be pathological. At any rate, to me they seem quite certain, and I shall assume that you agree with me in this. Without this assumption, we are in danger of falling into that universal scepticism which, as we saw, is as barren as it is irrefutable. If we are to continue philosophizing, we must make our bow to the sceptical hypothesis, and, while admitting the elegant terseness of its philosophy, proceed to the consideration of other hypotheses which, though perhaps not certain, have at least as good a right to our respect as the hypothesis of the sceptic.

Applying our distinction of " hard " and " soft " data to psychologically derivative but logically primitive beliefs, we shall find that most, if not all, are to be classed as soft data. They may be found, on reflection, to be capable of logical proof, and they then again become believed, but no longer as data. As data, though entitled to a certain limited respect, they cannot be placed on a level with the facts of sense or the laws of logic. The kind of respect which they deserve seems to me such as to warrant us in hoping, though not too confidently, that the hard data may prove them

to be at least probable. Also, if the hard data are
found to throw no light whatever upon their truth or
falsehood, we are justified, I think, in giving rather
more weight to the hypothesis of their truth than to
the hypothesis of their falsehood. For the present,
however, let us confine ourselves to the hard data,
with a view to discovering what sort of world can be
constructed by their means alone.

Our data now are primarily the facts of sense (i.e.
of *our own* sense-data) and the laws of logic. But even
the severest scrutiny will allow some additions to this
slender stock. Some facts of memory—especially
of recent memory—seem to have the highest degree of
certainty. Some introspective facts are as certain as
any facts of sense. And facts of sense themselves must,
for our present purposes, be interpreted with a certain
latitude. Spatial and temporal relations must sometimes be included, for example in the case of a swift
motion falling wholly within the specious present.
And some facts of comparison, such as the likeness
or unlikeness of two shades of colour, are certainly
to be included among hard data. Also we must remember that the distinction of hard and soft data is psychological and subjective, so that, if there are other
minds than our own—which at our present stage must
be held doubtful—the catalogue of hard data may be
different for them from what it is for us.

Certain common beliefs are undoubtedly excluded
from hard data. Such is the belief which led us to
introduce the distinction, namely, that sensible objects
in general persist when we are not perceiving them.
Such also is the belief in other people's minds : this
belief is psychologically derivative from our perception
of their bodies, and is felt to demand logical justification as soon as we become aware of its derivativeness.

Belief in what is reported by the testimony of others, including all that we learn from books, is of course involved in the doubt as to whether other people have minds at all. Thus the world from which our reconstruction is to begin is very fragmentary. The best we can say for it is that it is slightly more extensive than the world at which Descartes arrived by a similar process, since that world contained nothing except himself and his thoughts.

We are now in a position to understand and state the problem of our knowledge of the external world, and to remove various misunderstandings which have obscured the meaning of the problem. The problem really is : Can the existence of anything other than our own hard data be inferred from the existence of those data ? But before considering this problem, let us briefly consider what the problem is *not*.

When we speak of the " external " world in this discussion, we must not mean " spatially external," unless " space " is interpreted in a peculiar and recondite manner. The immediate objects of sight, the coloured surfaces which make up the visible world, are spatially external in the natural meaning of this phrase. We feel them to be " there " as opposed to " here " ; without making any assumption of an existence other than hard data, we can more or less estimate the distance of a coloured surface. It seems probable that distances, provided they are not too great, are actually given more or less roughly in sight ; but whether this is the case or not, ordinary distances can certainly be estimated approximately by means of the data of sense alone. The immediately given world is spatial, and is further not wholly contained within our own bodies, at least in the obvious sense.

Thus our knowledge of what is external in this sense is not open to doubt.

Another form in which the question is often put is : " Can we know of the existence of any reality which is independent of ourselves ? " This form of the question suffers from the ambiguity of the two words " independent " and " self." To take the Self first : the question as to what is to be reckoned part of the Self and what is not, is a very difficult one. Among many other things which we may mean by the Self, two may be selected as specially important, namely (1) the bare subject which thinks and is aware of objects, (2) the whole assemblage of things that would necessarily cease to exist if our lives came to an end. The bare subject, if it exists at all, is an inference, and is not part of the data ; therefore, this meaning of Self may be ignored in our present inquiry. The second meaning is difficult to make precise, since we hardly know what things depend upon our lives for their existence. And in this form, the definition of Self introduces the word " depend," which raises the same questions as are raised by the word " independent." Let us therefore take up the word " independent," and return to the Self later.

When we say that one thing is " independent " of another, we may mean either that it is logically possible for the one to exist without the other, or that there is no causal relation between the two such that the one only occurs as the effect of the other. The only way, so far as I know, in which one thing can be *logically* dependent upon another is when the other is *part* of the one. The existence of a book, for example, is logically dependent upon that of its pages : without the pages there would be no book. Thus in this sense the question, " Can we know of the existence of any reality which is independent of ourselves ? " reduces to the question, " Can we know of the existence of any reality of which our Self is not part ? " In this form, the question brings us back to the problem of defining the Self ; but I think, however the Self may be defined, even when it is taken as the bare subject, it cannot be supposed to be part of the immediate object of sense ; thus in this form of the question we must admit that we can know of the existence of realities independent of ourselves.

The question of causal dependence is much more difficult. To know that one kind of thing is causally independent of another, we must know that it actually occurs without the other. Now it is fairly obvious that, whatever legitimate meaning we give to the Self, our thoughts and feelings are causally dependent upon ourselves, i.e. do not occur when there is no Self for them to belong to. But in the case of objects of sense this is not obvious ; indeed, as we saw, the common-sense view is that such objects persist in the absence of any percipient. If this is the case, then they are causally independent of ourselves ; if not, not. Thus in this form the question reduces to the question whether we can know that objects of sense, or any other objects not our own thoughts and feelings, exist at times when we are not perceiving them. This form, in which the difficult word " independent " no longer occurs, is the form in which we stated the problem a minute ago.

Our question in the above form raises two distinct problems, which it is important to keep separate. First, can we know that objects of sense, or very similar objects, exist at times when we are not perceiving them ? Secondly, if this cannot be known, can we know that other objects, inferable from objects of sense but not necessarily resembling them, exist either when we are perceiving the objects of sense or at any other time ? This latter problem arises in philosophy as the problem of the " thing in itself," and in science as the problem of matter as assumed in physics. We will consider this latter problem first.

According to some authors—among whom I was formerly included—it is necessary to distinguish between a sensation, which is a mental event, and its object, which is a patch of colour or a noise or what not. If this distinction is made, the object of the sensation is called a " sense-datum " or a " sensible object." Nothing in the problems to be discussed in this book depends upon the question whether this distinction is valid or not. If it is not valid, the sensation and the sense-datum are identical. If it is valid, it is the sense-datum which concerns us in this book, not the sensation. For reasons explained in *The Analysis of Mind* (e.g. p. 141 ff.) I have come to regard the distinction as not valid, and to consider the sense-datum identical with the sensation. But it will not be necessary to assume the correctness of this view in what follows.

When I speak of a " sensible object," it must be understood that I do not mean such a thing as a table, which is both visible and tangible, can be seen by many people at once, and is more or less permanent. What I mean is just that patch of colour which is momentarily seen when we look at the table, or just that particular hardness which is felt when we press it, or just that particular sound which is heard when we rap it. Both the thing-in-itself of philosophy and the matter of physics present themselves as causes of the sensible object as much as of the sensation (if these are distinct). What are the common grounds for this opinion ?

In each case, I think, the opinion has resulted from the combination of a belief that *something* which can persist independently of our consciousness makes itself known in sensation, with the fact that our sensations often change in ways which seem to depend upon us rather than upon anything which would be supposed to persist independently of us. At first, we believe unreflectingly that everything is as it seems to be, and that, if we shut our eyes, the objects we had been seeing remain as they were though we no longer see them. But there are arguments against this view, which have generally been thought conclusive. It is extraordinarily difficult to see just what the arguments prove ; but if we are to make any progress with the problem of the external world, we must try to make up our minds as to these arguments.

A table viewed from one place presents a different appearance from that which it presents from another place. This is the language of common sense, but this language already assumes that there is a real table of which we see the appearances. Let us try to state what is known in terms of sensible objects alone, without any element of hypothesis. We find that as we walk round the table, we perceive a series of gradually changing visible objects. But in speaking of " walking round the table," we have still retained the hypothesis that there is a single table connected with all the appearances. What we ought to say is that, while we have those muscular and other sensations which make us say we are walking, our visual sensations change in a continuous way, so that, for example, a striking patch of colour is not suddenly replaced by

something wholly different, but is replaced by an
insensible gradation of slightly different colours with
slightly different shapes. This is what we really know
by experience, when we have freed our minds from
the assumption of permanent " things " with changing
appearances. What is really known is a correlation of
muscular and other bodily sensations with changes
in visual sensations.

But walking round the table is not the only way of
altering its appearance. We can shut one eye, or put
on blue spectacles, or look through a microscope.
All these operations, in various ways, alter the visual
appearance which we call that of the table. More
distant objects will also alter their appearance if (as
we say) the state of the atmosphere changes—if there
is fog or rain or sunshine. Physiological changes also
alter the appearances of things. If we assume the
world of common sense, all these changes, including
those attributed to physiological causes, are changes
in the intervening medium. It is not quite so easy as in
the former case to reduce this set of facts to a form
in which nothing is assumed beyond sensible objects.
Anything intervening between ourselves and what we
see must be invisible : our view in every direction is
bounded by the nearest visible object. It might
be objected that a dirty pane of glass, for example,
is visible, although we can see things through it. But
in this case we really see a spotted patchwork : the
dirtier specks in the glass are visible, while the cleaner
parts are invisible and allow us to see what is beyond.
Thus the discovery that the intervening medium affects
the appearances of things cannot be made by means of
the sense of sight alone.

Let us take the case of the blue spectacles, which is
the simplest, but may serve as a type for the others.

The frame of the spectacles is of course visible, but the blue glass, if it is clean, is not visible. The blueness, which we say is in the glass, appears as being in the objects seen through the glass. The glass itself is known by means of the sense of touch. In order to know that it is between us and the objects seen through it, we must know how to correlate the space of touch with the space of sight. This correlation itself, when stated in terms of the data of sense alone, is by no means a simple matter. But it presents no difficulties of principle, and may therefore be supposed accomplished. When it has been accomplished, it becomes possible to attach a meaning to the statement that the blue glass, which we can touch, is between us and the object seen, as we say, " through " it.

But we have still not reduced our statement completely to what is actually given in sense. We have fallen into the assumption that the object of which we are conscious when we touch the blue spectacles still exists after we have ceased to touch them. So long as we are touching them, nothing except our finger can be seen through the part touched, which is the only part where we immediately know that there is something. If we are to account for the blue appearance of objects other than the spectacles, when seen through them, it might seem as if we must assume that the spectacles still exist when we are not touching them ; and if this assumption really is necessary, our main problem is answered : we have means of knowing of the present existence of objects not given in sense, though of the same kind as objects formerly given in sense.

It may be questioned, however, whether this assumption is actually unavoidable, though it is unquestionably the most natural one to make. We may say that the

object of which we become aware when we touch the
spectacles continues to have effects afterwards, though
perhaps it no longer exists. In this view, the supposed
continued existence of sensible objects after they have
ceased to be sensible will be a fallacious inference
from the fact that they still have effects. It is often
supposed that nothing which has ceased to exist can
continue to have effects, but this is a mere prejudice, due to a wrong conception of causality. We
cannot, therefore, dismiss our present hypothesis
on the ground of *a priori* impossibility, but must
examine further whether it can really account for
the facts.

It may be said that our hypothesis is useless in the
case when the blue glass is never touched at all. How,
in that case, are we to account for the blue appearance
of objects ? And more generally, what are we to make
of the hypothetical sensations of touch which we
associate with untouched visible objects, which we
know would be verified if we chose, though in fact we
do not verify them ? Must not these be attributed to
permanent possession, by the objects, of the properties
which touch would reveal ?

Let us consider the more general question first.
Experience has taught us that where we see certain
kinds of coloured surfaces we can, by touch, obtain
certain expected sensations of hardness or softness,
tactile shape, and so on. This leads us to believe that
what is seen is usually tangible, and that it has, whether
we touch it or not, the hardness or softness which we
should expect to feel if we touched it. But the mere
fact that we are able to infer what our tactile sensations
would be shows that it is not logically necessary to
assume tactile qualities before they are felt. All that
is really known is that the visual appearance in question

together with touch, will lead to certain sensations, which can necessarily be determined in terms of the visual appearance, since otherwise they could not be inferred from it.

We can now give a statement of the experienced facts concerning the blue spectacles, which will supply an interpretation of common-sense beliefs without assuming anything beyond the existence of sensible objects at the times when they are sensible. By experience of the correlation of touch and sight sensations, we become able to associate a certain place in touch-space with a certain corresponding place in sight-space. Sometimes, namely in the case of transparent things, we find that there is a tangible object in a touch-place without there being any visible object in the corresponding sight-place. But in such a case as that of the blue spectacles, we find that whatever object is visible beyond the empty sight-place in the same line of sight has a different colour from what it has when there is no tangible object in the intervening touch-place ; and as we move the tangible object in touch-space, the blue patch moves in sight-space. If now we find a blue patch moving in this way in sight-space, when we have no sensible experience of an intervening tangible object, we nevertheless infer that, if we put our hand at a certain place in touch-space, we should experience a certain touch-sensation. If we are to avoid non-sensible objects, this must be taken as the whole of our meaning when we say that the blue spectacles are in a certain place, though we have not touched them, and have only seen other things rendered blue by their interposition.

I think it may be laid down quite generally that, *in so far* as physics or common sense is verifiable, it must be capable of interpretation in terms of actual sense-data alone. The reason for this is simple. Verification consists always in the occurrence of an expected sense-datum. Astronomers tell us there will be an eclipse of the moon : we look at the moon, and find the earth's shadow biting into it, that is to say, we see an appearance quite different from that of the usual full moon. Now if an expected sense-datum constitutes a verification, what was asserted must have been about sense-data ; or, at any rate, if part of what was asserted was not about sense-data, then only the other part has been verified. There is in fact a certain regularity or conformity to law about the occurrence of sense-data, but the sense-data that occur at one time are often causally connected with those that occur at quite other times, and not, or at least not very closely, with those that occur at neighbouring times. If I look at the moon and immediately afterwards hear a train coming, there is no very close causal connection between my two sense-data ; but if I look at the moon on two nights a week apart, there is a very close causal connection between the two sense-data. The simplest, or at least the easiest, statement of the connection is obtained by imagining a " real " moon which goes on whether I look at it or not, providing a series of *possible* sense-data of which only those are actual which belongs to moments when I choose to look at the moon.

But the degree of verification obtainable in this way is very small. It must be remembered that, at our present level of doubt, we are not at liberty to accept testimony. When we hear certain noises, which are those we should utter if we wished to express a certain thought, we assume that that thought, or one very like it, has been in another mind, and has given rise to the expression which we hear. If at the same time we see a body resembling our own, moving its lips as we move ours when we speak, we cannot resist the belief that it is alive, and that the feelings inside it continue when we are not looking at it. When we see our friend drop a weight upon his toe, and hear him say—what we should say in similar circumstances, the phenomena *can* no doubt be explained without assuming that he is anything but a series of shapes and noises seen and heard by us, but practically no man is so infected with philosophy as not to be quite certain that his friend has felt the same kind of pain as he himself would feel. We will consider the legitimacy of this belief presently ; for the moment, I only wish to point out that it needs the same kind of justification as our belief that the moon exists when we do not see it, and that, without it, testimony heard or read is reduced to noises and shapes, and cannot be regarded as evidence of the facts which it reports. The verification of physics which is possible at our present level is, therefore, only that degree of verification which is possible by one man's unaided observations, which will not carry us very far towards the establishment of a whole science.

Before proceeding further, let us summarize the argument so far as it has gone. The problem is : " Can the existence of anything other than our own hard data be inferred from these data ? " It is a mistake to state the problem in the form : " Can we know of the existence of anything other than ourselves and our states ? " or : " Can we know of the existence of anything independent of ourselves ? " because of the extreme difficulty of defining " self " and " independent " precisely. The felt passivity of sensation is irrelevant, since, even if it proved anything, it could only prove that sensations are caused by sensible objects. The natural *naïve* belief is that things seen persist, when unseen, exactly or approximately as they appeared when seen ; but this belief tends to be dispelled by the fact that what common sense regards as the appearance of one object changes with what common sense regards as changes in the point of view and in the intervening medium, including in the latter our own sense-organs and nerves and brain. This fact, as just stated, assumes, however, the common-sense world of stable objects which it professes to call in question ; hence, before we can discover its precise bearing on our problem, we must find a way of stating it which does not involve any of the assumptions which it is designed to render doubtful. What we then find, as the bare outcome of experience, is that gradual changes in certain sense-data are correlated with gradual changes in certain others, or (in the case of bodily motions) with the other sense-data themselves.

The assumption that sensible objects persist after they have ceased to be sensible—for example, that the hardness of a visible body, which has been discovered by touch, continues when the body is no longer touched—may be replaced by the statement that the *effects* of sensible objects persist, i.e. that what happens now can only be accounted for, in many cases, by taking account of what happened at an earlier time. Everything that one man, by his own personal experience, can verify in the account of the world given by common sense and physics, will be explicable by some such means, since verification consists merely in the occurrence of an expected sense-datum. But what depends upon testimony, whether heard or read, cannot be explained in this way, since testimony depends upon the existence of minds other than our own, and thus requires a knowledge of something not given in sense. But before examining the question of our knowledge of other minds, let us return to the question of the thing-in-itself, namely, to the theory that what exists at times when we are not perceiving a given sensible object is something quite unlike that object, something which, together with us and our sense-organs, causes our sensations, but is never itself given in sensation.

The thing-in-itself, when we start from common-sense assumptions, is a fairly natural outcome of the difficulties due to the changing appearances of what is supposed to be one object. It is supposed that the table (for example) causes our sense-data of sight and touch, but must, since these are altered by the point of view and the intervening medium, be quite different from the sense-data to which it gives rise. The objection to this theory, I think, lies in its failure to realize the radical nature of the reccnstruction demanded by the difficulties to which it points. We cannot speak legitimately of changes in the point of view and the intervening medium until we have already constructed some world more stable than that of momentary sensation. Our discussion of the blue spectacles and the walk round the table has, I hope, made this clear. But what remains far from clear is the nature of the reconstruction required.

Although we cannot rest content with the above theory, in the terms in which it is stated, we must nevertheless treat it with a certain respect, for it is in outline the theory upon which physical science and physiology are built, and it must, therefore, be suscep-tible of a true interpretation. Let us see how this is to be done.

The first thing to realize is that there are no such

things as " illusions of sense." Objects of sense, even when they occur in dreams, are the most indubitably real objects known to us. What, then, makes us call them unreal in dreams ? Merely the unusual nature of their connection with other objects of sense. I dream that I am in America, but I wake up and find myself in England without those intervening days on the Atlantic which, alas ! are inseparably connected with a " real " visit to America. Objects of sense are called " real " when they have the kind of connection with other objects of sense which experience has led us to regard as normal ; when they fail in this, they are called " illusions." But what is illusory is only the inferences to which they give rise ; in themselves, they are every bit as real as the objects of waking life. And conversely, the sensible objects of waking life must not be expected to have any more intrinsic reality than those of dreams. Dreams and waking life, in our first efforts at construction, must be treated with equal respect ; it is only by some reality not *merely* sensible that dreams can be condemned.

Accepting the indubitable momentary reality of objects of sense, the next thing to notice. is the confusion underlying objections derived from their changeableness. As we walk round the table, its aspect changes ; but it is thought impossible to maintain either that the table changes, or that its various aspects can all " really " exist in the same place. If we press one eyeball, we shall see two tables ; but it is thought preposterous to maintain that there are " really " two tables. Such arguments, however, seem to involve the assumption that there can be something more real than objects of sense. If we see two tables, then there *are* two visual tables. It is perfectly true that, at the same moment, we may discover by touch that there is only one tactile table. This makes us declare the two visual tables an illusion, because usually one visual object corresponds to one tactile object. But all that we are warranted in saying is that, in this case, the manner of correlation of touch and sight is unusual. Again, when the aspect of the table changes as we walk round it, and we are told there cannot be so many different aspects in the same place, the answer is simple : what does the critic of the table mean by " the same place " ? The use of such a phrase presupposes that all our difficulties have been solved ; as yet, we have no right to speak of a " place " except with reference to one given set of momentary sense-data. When all are changed by a bodily movement, no place remains the same as it was. Thus the difficulty, if it exists, has at least not been rightly stated.

We will now make a new start, adopting a different method. Instead of inquiring what is the minimum of assumption by which we can explain the world of sense, we will, in order to have a model hypothesis as a help for the imagination, construct one possible (not necessary) explanation of the facts. It may perhaps then be possible to pare away what is superfluous in our hypothesis, leaving a residue which may be regarded as the abstract answer to our problem.

Let us imagine that each mind looks out upon the world, as in Leibniz's monadology, from a point of view peculiar to itself ; and for the sake of simplicity let us confine ourselves to the sense of sight, ignoring minds which are devoid of this sense. Each mind sees at each moment an immensely complex three-dimensional world ; but there is absolutely nothing which is seen by two minds simultaneously. When we say that two people see the same thing, we always find that, owing to difference of point of view, there are differences, however slight, between their immediate sensible objects. (I am here assuming the validity of testimony but as we are only constructing a *possible* theory, that is a legitimate assumption.) The three-dimensional world seen by one mind therefore contains no place in common with that seen by another, for places can only be constituted by the things in or around them. Hence we may suppose, in spite of the differences between the different worlds, that each exists entire exactly as it is perceived, and might be exactly as it is even if it were not perceived. We may further suppose that there are an infinite number of such worlds which are in fact unperceived. If two men are sitting in a room, two somewhat similar worlds are perceived by them ; if a third man enters and sits between them, a third world, intermediate between the two previous worlds, begins to be perceived. It is true that we cannot reasonably suppose just this world to have existed before, because it is conditioned by the sense-organs, nerves, and brain of the newly arrived man ; but we can reasonably suppose that *some* aspect of the universe existed from that point of view, though no one was perceiving it. The system consisting of all views of the universe, perceived and unperceived, I shall call the system of "perspectives"; I shall confine the expression "private worlds" to such views of the universe as are actually perceived. Thus a "private world" is a perceived "perspective" but there may be any number of unperceived perspectives.

Two men are sometimes found to perceive very similar perspectives, so similar that they can use the same words to describe them. They say they see the same table, because the differences between the two tables they see are slight and not practically important. Thus it is possible, sometimes, to establish a correlation by similarity between a great many of the things of one perspective, and a great many of the things of another. In case the similarity is very great, we say the points of view of the two perspectives are near together in space ; but this space in which they are near together is totally different from the spaces inside the two perspectives. It is a relation between the perspectives, and is not in either of them ; no one can perceive it, and if it is to be known it can be only by inference. Between two perceived perspectives which are similar, we can imagine a whole series of other perspectives, some at least unperceived, and such that between any two, however similar, there are others still more similar. In this way the space which consists of relations between perspectives can be rendered continuous, and (if we choose) three-dimensional.

We can now define the momentary common-sense " thing," as opposed to its momentary appearances. By the similarity of neighbouring perspectives, many objects in the one can be correlated with objects in the other, namely with the similar objects. Given an object in one perspective, form the system of all the objects correlated with it in all the perspectives ; that system may be identified with the momentary common-sense " thing." Thus an aspect of a " thing " is a member of the system of aspects which *is* the " thing " at that moment. (The correlation of the times of different perspectives raises certain complications, of the kind considered in the theory of relativity ; but we may ignore these at present.) All the aspects of a thing are real, whereas the thing is a merely logical construction. It has, however, the merit of being neutral as between different points of view, and of being visible to more than one person, in the only sense in which it can ever be visible, namely, in the sense that each sees one of its aspects.

It will be observed that, while each perspective contains its own space, there is only one space in which the perspectives themselves are the elements. There are as many private spaces as there are perspectives ; there are therefore at least as many as there are percipients, and there may be any number of others which have a merely material existence and are not seen by anyone. But there is only one perspective-space, whose elements are single perspectives, each with its own private space. We have now to explain how the private space of a single perspective is correlated with part of the one all-embracing perspective space.

Perspective space is the system of " points of view " of private spaces (perspectives), or, since " points of view " have not been defined, we may say it is the system of the private spaces themselves. These private spaces will each count as one point, or at any rate as one element, in perspective space. They are ordered by means of their similarities. Suppose, for example, that we start from one which contains the appearance of a circular disc, such as would be called a penny, and suppose this appearance, in the perspective in question, is circular, not elliptic. We can then form a whole series of perspectives containing a graduated series of circular aspects of varying sizes : for this purpose we only have to move (as we say) towards the penny or away from it. The perspectives in which the penny looks circular will be said to lie on a straight line in perspective space, and their order on this line will be that of the sizes of the circular aspects. Moreover—though this statement must be noticed and subsequently examined—the perspectives in which the penny looks big will be said to be nearer to the penny than those in which it looks small. It is to be remarked also that any other " thing " than our penny might have been chosen to define the relations of our perspectives in perspective space, and that experience shows that the same spatial order of perspectives would have resulted.

In order to explain the correlation of private spaces with perspective space, we have first to explain what is meant by " the place (in perspective space) where a thing is." For this purpose, let us again consider the penny which appears in many perspectives. We formed a straight line of perspectives in which the penny looked circular, and we agreed that those in which it looked larger were to be considered as nearer to the penny. We can form another straight line of perspectives in which the penny is seen end-on and looks like a straight line of a certain thickness. These two lines will meet in a certain place in perspective space, i.e. in a certain perspective, which may be defined as " the place (in perspective space) where the penny is." It is true that, in order to prolong our lines until they reach this place, we shall have to make use of other things besides the penny, because, so far as experience goes, the penny ceases to present any appearance after we have come so near to it that it touches the eye. But this raises no real difficulty, because the spacial order of perspectives is found empirically to be independent of the particular " things " chosen for defining the order. We can, for example, remove our penny and prolong each of our two straight lines up to their intersection by placing other pennies further off in such a way that the aspects of the one are circular where those of our original penny were circular, and the aspects of the other are straight where those of our original penny were straight. There will then be just one perspective in which one of the new pennies looks circular and the other straight. This will be, by definition, the place where the original penny was in perspective space.

The above is, of course, only a first rough sketch of the way in which our definition is to be reached. It neglects the size of the penny, and it assumes that we can remove the penny without being disturbed by any simultaneous changes in the positions of other things. But it is plain that such niceties cannot affect the principle, and can only introduce complications in its application.

Having now defined the perspective, which is the place where a given thing is, we can understand what is meant by saying that the perspectives in which a think looks large are nearer to the things than those in which it looks small: they are, in fact, nearer to the perspective which is the place where the thing is.

We can now also explain the correlation between a private space and parts of perspective space. If there is an aspect of a given thing in a certain private space, then we correlate the place where this aspect is in the private space with the place where the thing is in perspective space.

We may define " here " as the place, in perspective space, which is occupied by our private world. Thus we can now understand what is meant by speaking of a thing as near to or far from " here." A thing is near to " here " if the place where it is is near to my private world. We can also understand what is meant by saying that our private world is inside our head ; for our private world is a place in perspective space, and may be part of the place where our head is.

It will be observed that *two* places in perspective space are associated with every aspect of a thing : namely, the place where the thing is, and the place which is the perspective of which the aspect in question forms part. Every aspect of a thing is a member of two different classes of aspects, namely : (1) the various aspects of the thing, of which at most one appears in any given perspective ; (2) the perspective of which the given aspect is a member, i.e. that in which the thing has the given aspect. The physicist naturally classifies aspects in the first way, the psychologist in the second. The two places associated with a single aspect correspond to the two ways of classifying it. We may distinguish the two places as that *at* which, and that *from* which, the aspect appears. The " place at which " is the place of the thing to which the aspect belongs ; the " place from which " is the place of the perspective to which the aspect belongs.

Let us now endeavour to state the fact that the aspect which a thing presents at a given place is affected by the intervening medium. The aspects of a thing in different perspectives are to be conceived as spreading outwards from the place where the thing is, and undergoing various changes as they get further away from this place. The laws according to which they change cannot be stated if we only take account of the aspects that are near the thing, but require that we should also take account of the things that are at the places from which these aspects appear. This empirical fact can, therefore, be interpreted in terms of our construction.

We have now constructed a largely hypothetical picture of the world, which contains and places the experienced facts, including those derived from testimony. The world we have constructed can, with a certain amount of trouble, be used to interpret the crude facts of sense, the facts of physics, and the facts of physiology. It is therefore a world which *may* be actual. It fits the facts, and there is no empirical evidence against it ; it also is free from logical impossibilities. But have we any good reason to suppose that it is real ? This brings us back to our original problem, as to the grounds for believing in the existence of anything outside my private world. What we have derived from our hypothetical construction is that there are no grounds *against* the truth of this belief, but we have not derived any positive grounds in its favour. We will resume this inquiry by taking up again the question of testimony and the evidence for the existence of other minds.

It must be conceded to begin with that the argument in favour of the existence of other people's minds cannot be conclusive. A phantasm of our dreams will appear to have a mind—a mind to be annoying, as a rule. It will give unexpected answers, refuse to conform to our desires, and show all those other signs of intelligence to which we are accustomed in the acquaintances of our waking hours. And yet, when we are awake, we do not believe that the phantasm was, like the appearances of people in waking life, representative of a private world to which we have no direct access. If we are to believe this of the people we meet when we are awake, it must be on some ground short of demonstration, since it is obviously possible that what we call waking life may be only an unusually persistent and recurrent nightmare. It may be that our imagination brings forth all that other people seem to say to us, all that we read in books, all the daily, weekly, monthly, and quarterly journals that distract our thoughts, all the advertisements of soap and all the speeches of politicians. This *may* be true, since it cannot be shown to be false, yet no one can really believe it. Is there any *logical* ground for regarding this possibility as improbable ? Or is there nothing beyond habit and prejudice ?

The minds of other people are among our data, in the very wide sense in which we used the word at first. That is to say, when we first begin to reflect, we find ourselves already believing in them, not because of any argument, but because the belief is natural to us. It is, however, a psychologically derivative belief, since it results from observation of people's bodies ; and along with other such beliefs, it does not belong to the hardest of hard data, but becomes, under the influence of philosophic reflection, just sufficiently questionable to make us desire some argument connecting it with the facts of sense.

The obvious argument is, of course, derived from analogy. Other people's bodies behave as ours do when we have certain thoughts and feelings ; hence, by analogy, it is natural to suppose that such behaviour is connected with thoughts and feelings like our own. Someone says " Look out ! " and we find we are on the point of being killed by a motor-car ; we therefore attribute the words we heard to the person in question having seen the motor-car first, in which case there are existing things of which we are not directly conscious. But this whole scene, with our inference, may occur in a dream, in which case the inference is generally considered to be mistaken. Is there anything to make the argument from analogy more cogent when we are (as we think) awake ?

The analogy in waking life is only to be preferred to

that in dreams on the ground of its greater extent and consistency. If a man were to dream every night about a set of people whom he never met by day, who had consistent characters and grew older with the lapse of years, he might, like the man in Calderon's play, find it difficult to decide which was the dream-world and which was the so-called " real " world. It is only the failure of our dreams to form a consistent whole either with each other or with waking life that makes us condemn them. Certain uniformities are observed in waking life, while dreams seem quite erratic. The natural hypothesis would be that demons and the spirits of the dead visit us while we sleep ; but the modern mind, as a rule, refuses to entertain this view, though it is hard to see what could be said against it. On the other hand, the mystic, in moments of illumination, seems to awaken from a sleep which has filled all his mundane life : the whole world of sense becomes phantasmal, and he sees, with the clarity and convincingness that belongs to our morning realization after dreams, a world utterly different from that of our daily cares and troubles. Who shall condemn him ? Who shall justify him ? Or who shall justify the seeming solidity of the common objects among which we suppose ourselves to live ?

The hypothesis that other people have minds must, I think, be allowed to be not susceptible of any very strong support from the analogical argument. At the same time, it is a hypothesis which systematizes a vast body of facts and never leads to any consequences which there is reason to think false. There is therefore nothing to be said against its truth, and good reason to use it as a working hypothesis. When once it is admitted, it enables us to extend our knowledge of the sensible world by testimony, and thus leads to the system of private worlds which we assumed in our hypothetical construction. In actual fact, whatever we may try to think as philosophers, we cannot help believing in the minds of other people, so that the question whether our belief is justified has a merely speculative interest. And if it is justified, then there is no further difficulty of principle in that vast extension of our knowledge, beyond our own private data, which we find in science and common sense.

This somewhat meagre conclusion must not be regarded as the whole outcome of our long discussion. The problem of the connection of sense with objective reality has commonly been dealt with from a standpoint which did not carry initial doubt so far as we have carried it ; most writers, consciously or unconsciously, have assumed that the testimony of others is to be admitted, and therefore (at least by implication) that others have minds. Their difficulties have arisen after this admission, from the differences in the appearance which one physical object presents to two people at the same time, or to one person at two times between which it cannot be supposed to have changed. Such difficulties have made people doubtful how far objective reality could be known by sense at all, and have made them suppose that there were positive arguments against the view that it can be so known. Our hypothetical construction meets these arguments, and shows that the account of the world given by common sense and physical science can be interpreted in a way which is logically unobjectionable, and finds a place for all the data, both hard and soft. It is this hypothetical construction, with its reconciliation of psychology and physics, which is the chief outcome of our discussion. Probably the construction is only in part necessary as an initial assumption, and can be obtained from more slender materials by the logical methods of which we shall have an example in the definitions of points, instants, and particles ; but I do not yet know to what lengths this diminution in our initial assumptions can be carried.

LECTURE IV

THE WORLD OF PHYSICS AND THE WORLD OF SENSE

AMONG the objections to the reality of objects of sense, there is one which is derived from the apparent difference between matter as it appears in physics and things as they appear in sensation. Men of science, for the most part, are willing to condemn immediate data as " merely subjective," while yet maintaining the truth of the physics inferred from those data. But such an attitude, though it may be *capable* of justification, obviously stands in need of it ; and the only justification possible must be one which exhibits matter as a logical construction from sense-data—unless, indeed, there were some wholly *a priori* principle by which unknown entities could be inferred from such as are known. It is therefore necessary to find some way of bridging the gulf between the world of physics and the world of sense, and it is this problem which will occupy us in the present lecture. Physicists appear to be unconscious of the gulf, while psychologists, who are conscious of it, have not the mathematical knowledge required for spanning it. The problem is difficult, and I do not know its solution in detail. All that I can hope to do is to make the problem felt, and to indicate the kind of methods by which a solution is to be sought.

Let us begin by a brief description of the two contrasted worlds. We will take first the world of physics, for, though the other world is given while the physical world is inferred, to us now the world of physics is the more familiar, the world of pure sense having become strange and difficult to rediscover. Physics started from the common-sense belief in fairly permanent and fairly rigid bodies—tables and chairs, stones, mountains, the earth and moon and sun. This common-sense belief, it should be noticed, is a piece of audacious metaphysical theorizing ; objects are not continually present to sensation, and it may be doubted whether they are there when they are not seen or felt. This problem, which has been acute since the time of Berkeley, is ignored by common sense, and has therefore hitherto been ignored by physicists. We have thus here a first departure from the immediate data of sensation, though it is a departure merely by way of extension, and was probably made by our savage ancestors in some very remote prehistoric epoch.

But tables and chairs, stones and mountains, are not *quite* permanent or *quite* rigid. Tables and chairs lose their legs, stones are split by frost, and mountains are cleft by earthquakes and eruptions. Then there are other things, which seem material, and yet present almost no permanence or rigidity. Breath, smoke, clouds, are examples of such things—so, in a lesser degree, are ice and snow ; and rivers and seas, though fairly permanent, are not in any degree rigid. Breath, smoke, clouds, and generally things that can be seen but not touched, were thought to be hardly real ; to this day the usual mark of a ghost is that it can be seen but not touched. Such objects were peculiar in the fact that they seemed to disappear completely, not merely to be transformed into something else. Ice and snow, when they disappear, are replaced by water ; and it required no great theoretical effort to invent the hypothesis that the water was the same thing as the ice and snow, but in a new form. Solid bodies, when they break, break into parts which are practically the same in shape and size as they were before. A stone can be hammered into a powder, but the powder consists of grains which retain the character they had before the pounding. Thus the ideal of absolutely rigid and absolutely permanent bodies, which early physicists pursued throughout the changing appearances, seemed attainable by supposing ordinary bodies to be composed of a vast number of tiny atoms. This billiard-ball view of matter dominated the imagination of physicists until quite modern times, until, in fact, it was replaced by the electromagnetic theory, which in its turn has developed into a new atomism. Apart from the special form of the atomic theory which was invented for the needs of chemistry, some kind of atomism dominated the whole of traditional dynamics, and was implied in every statement of its laws and axioms.

The modern form of atomism regards all matter as composed of two kinds of units, electrons and protons, both indestructible. All electrons, so far as we can discover, are exactly alike, and so are all protons. In addition to this form of atomicity, which is not very different from that of the Greeks except in being based upon experimental evidence, there is a wholly new form, introduced by the theory of quanta. Here the indivisible unit is a unit of " action," i.e. energy multiplied by time, or mass multiplied by length multiplied by velocity. This is not at all the sort of quantity in which traditional notions had led us to expect atomicity. But relativity makes this kind of atomicity less surprising, although so far it cannot deduce any form of atomicity, either old or new, from its fundamental axioms. Relativity has introduced a wholly novel analysis of physical concepts, and has made it easier than it formerly was to build a bridge from physics to sense-data. To make this clear, it will be necessary to say something about relativity. But before doing so, let us examine our problem from the other end, namely that of sense-data.

In the world of immediate data nothing is permanent ; even the things that we regard as fairly permanent, such as mountains, only become data when we see them, and are not immediately given as existing at other moments. So far from one all-embracing space being given, there are several spaces for each person, according to the different senses which may be called spatial. Experience teaches us to obtain one space from these by correlation, and experience, together with instinctive theorizing, teaches us to correlate our spaces with those which we believe to exist in the sensible world of other people. The construction of a single time offers less difficulty so long as we confine ourselves to one person's private world, but the correlation of one private time with another is a matter of great difficulty. While engaged in the necessary logical constructions, we can console ourselves with the knowledge that permanent things, space, and time have ceased to be, for relativity physics, part of the bare bones of the world, and are now admitted to be constructions. In attempting to construct them from sense-data and particulars structurally analogous to sense-data, we are, therefore, only pushing the procedure of relativity theory one stage further back.

The belief in indestructible "things" very early took the form of atomism. The underlying motive in atomism was not, I think, any empirical success in interpreting phenomena, but rather an instinctive belief that beneath all the changes of the sensible world there must be something permanent and unchanging. This belief was, no doubt, fostered and nourished by its practical successes, culminating in the conservation of mass ; but it was not produced by these successes. On the contrary, they were produced by it. Philosophical writers on physics sometimes speak as though the conservation of something or other were essential to the possibility of science, but this, I believe, is an entirely erroneous opinion. If the *a priori* belief in permanence had not existed, the same laws which are now formulated in terms of this belief might just as well have been formulated without it. Why should we suppose that, when ice melts, the water which replaces it is the same thing in a new form ? Merely because this supposition enables us to state the phenomena in a way which is consonant with our prejudices. What we really know is that, under certain conditions of temperature, the appearance we call ice is replaced by the appearance we call water. We can give laws according to which the one appearance will be succeeded by the other, but there is no reason except prejudice for regarding both as appearances of the same substance.

One task, if what has just been said is correct, which confronts us in trying to connect the world of sense with the world of physics, is the task of reconstructing the conception of matter without the *a priori* beliefs which historically gave rise to it. In spite of the revolutionary results of modern physics, the empirical successes of the conception of matter show that there must be some legitimate conception which fulfils roughly the same functions. The time has hardly come when we can state precisely what this legitimate conception is, but we can see in a general way what it must be like. For this purpose, it is only necessary to take our ordinary common-sense statements and reword them without the assumption of permanent substance. We say, for example, that things change gradually—sometimes very quickly, but not without passing through a continuous series of intermediate states, or at least an approximately continuous series, if the discontinuities of the quantum theory should prove ultimate. What this means is that, given any sensible appearance, there will usually be, *if we watch*, a continuous series of appearances connected with the given one, leading on by imperceptible gradations to the new appearances which common sense regards as those of the same thing. Thus a thing may be defined as a certain series of appearances, connected with each other by continuity and by certain causal laws. In the case of slowly changing things, this is easily seen. Consider, say, a wall-paper which fades in the course of years. It is an effort not to conceive of it as one " thing " whose colour is slightly different at one time from what it is at another. But what do we really *know* about it ? We know that under suitable circumstances—i.e. when we are, as is said, " in the room "—we perceive certain colours in a certain pattern : not always precisely the same colours, but sufficiently similar to feel familiar. If we can state the laws according to which the colour varies, we can state all that is empirically verifiable ; the assumption that there is a constant entity, the wall-paper, which " has " these various colours at various times, is a piece of gratuitous metaphysics. We may, if we like, *define* the wall-paper as the series of its aspects. These are collected together by the same motives which led us to regard the wall-paper as one thing, namely a combination of sensible continuity and causal connection. More generally, a " thing " will be defined as a certain series of aspects, namely those which would commonly be said to be *of* the thing. To say that a certain aspect is an aspect *of* a certain thing will merely mean that it is one of those which, taken serially, *are* the thing. Everything will then proceed as before : whatever was verifiable is unchanged, but our language is so interpreted as to avoid an unnecessary metaphysical assumption of permanence.

The above extrusion of permanent things affords an example of the maxim which inspires all scientific philosophizing, namely " Occam's razor " : *Entities are not to be multiplied without necessity.* In other words, in dealing with any subject-matter, find out what entities are undeniably involved, and state everything in terms of these entities. Very often the resulting statement is more complicated and difficult than one which, like common sense and most philosophy, assumes hypothetical entities whose existence there is no good reason to believe in. We find it easier to imagine a wall-paper with changing colours than to think merely of the series of colours ; but it is a mistake to suppose that what is easy and natural in thought is what is most free from unwarrantable assumptions, as the case of " things " very aptly illustrates.

The above summary account of the genesis of " things," though it may be correct in outline, has omitted some serious difficulties which it is necessary briefly to consider. Starting from a world of helter-skelter sense-data, we wish to collect them into series, each of which can be regarded as consisting of the successive appearances of one " thing." There is, to begin with, some conflict between what common sense regards as one thing, and what physics regards an unchanging collection of particles. To common sense, a human body is one thing, but to science the matter composing it is continually changing. This conflict, however, is not very serious, and may, for our rough preliminary purpose, be largely ignored. The problem is : by what principles shall we select certain data from the chaos, and call them all appearances of the same thing ?

A rough and approximate answer to this question is not very difficult. There are certain fairly stable collections of appearances, such as landscapes, the furniture of rooms, the faces of acquaintances. In these cases, we have little hesitation in regarding them on successive occasions as appearances of one thing or collection of things. But, as the *Comedy of Errors* illustrates, we may be led astray if we judge by mere resemblance. This shows that something more is involved, for two different things may have any degree of likeness up to exact similarity.

Another insufficient criterion of one thing is *continuity*. As we have already seen, if we watch what we regard as one changing thing, we usually find its changes to be continuous so far as our senses can perceive. We are thus led to assume that, if we see two finitely different appearances at two different times, and if we have reason to regard them as belonging to the same thing, then there was a continuous series of intermediate states of that thing during the time when we were not observing it. And so it comes to be thought that continuity of change is necessary and sufficient to constitute one thing. But in fact it is neither. It is not *necessary*, because the unobserved states, in the case where our attention has not been concentrated on the thing throughout, are purely hypothetical, and cannot possibly be our ground for supposing the earlier and later appearances to belong to the same thing ; on the contrary, it is because we suppose this that we assume intermediate unobserved states. Continuity is also not sufficient, since we can, for example, pass by sensibly continuous gradations from any one drop of the sea to any other drop. The utmost we can say is that discontinuity during un-interrupted observation is as a rule a mark of difference between things, though even this cannot be said in such cases as sudden explosions. (We are speaking throughout of the immediate sensible appearance, counting as continuous whatever *seems* continuous, and as discontinuous whatever *seems* discontinuous.)

The assumption of continuity is, however, success-fully made in physics. This proves something, though not anything of very obvious utility to our present problem : it proves that nothing in the known world (apart, possibly, from quantum phenomena) is incon-sistent with the hypothesis that all changes are really continuous, though from too great rapidity or from our lack of observation they may not always appear continuous. In this hypothetical sense, continuity or change which, though sudden, is in accordance with quantum principles, may be allowed to be a *necessary* conidtion if two appearances are to be classed as appearances of the same thing. But it is not a *sufficient* condition, as appears from the instances of the drops in the sea. Thus something more must be sought before we can give even the roughest definition of a " thing."

What is wanted further seems to be something in the nature of fulfilment of causal laws. This statement, as it stands, is very vague, but we will endeavour to give it precision. When I speak of "causal laws," I mean any laws which connect events at different times, or even, as a limiting case, events at the same time provided the connection is not logically demonstrable. In this very general sense, the laws of dynamics are causal laws, and so are the laws correlating the simultaneous appearances of one "thing" to different senses. The question is : How do such laws help in the definition of a "thing"?

To answer this question, we must consider what it is that is proved by the empirical success of physics. What is proved is that its hypotheses, though unverifiable where they go beyond sense-data, are at no point in contradiction with sense-data, but, on the contrary, are ideally such as to render all sense-data calculable from a sufficient collection of data all belonging to a given period of time. Now physics has found it empirically possible to collect sense-data into series, each series being regarded as belonging to one "thing," and behaving, with regard to the laws of physics, in a way in which series not belonging to one thing would in general not behave. If it is to be unambiguous whether two appearances belong to the same thing or not, there must be only one way of grouping appearances so that the resulting things obey the laws of physics. It would be very difficult to prove that this is the case, but for our present purposes we may let this point pass, and assume that there is only one way. We must include in our definition of a "thing" those of its aspects, if any, which are not observed. Thus we may lay down the following definition : *Things are those series of aspects which obey the laws of physics.* That such series exist is an empirical fact, which constitutes the verifiability of physics.

It may still be objected that the "matter" of physics is something other than series of sense-data. Sense-data, it may be said, belong to psychology and are, at any rate in some sense, subjective, whereas physics is quite independent of psychological considerations, and does not assume that its matter only exists when it is perceived.

To this objection there are two answers, both of some importance.

(*a*) We have been considering, in the above account, the question of the *verifiability* of physics. Now verifiability is by no means the same thing as truth ; it is, in fact, something far more subjective and psychological. For a proposition to be verifiable, it is not enough that it should be true, but it must also be such as we can *discover* to be true. Thus verifiability depends upon our capacity for acquiring knowledge, and not only upon the objective truth. In physics, as ordinarily set forth, there is much that is unverifiable : there are hypotheses as to (α) how things would appear to a spectator in a place where, as it happens, there is no spectator ; (β) how things would appear at times when, in fact, they are not appearing to anyone ; (γ) things which never appear at all. All these are introduced to simplify the statement of the causal laws, but none of them form an integral part of what is *known* to be true in physics. This brings us to our second answer.

(*b*) If physics is to consist wholly of propositions known to be true, or at least capable of being proved or disproved, the three kinds of hypothetical entities we have just enumerated must all be capable of being exhibited as logical functions of sense-data. In order to show how this might possibly be done, let us recall the hypothetical Leibnizian universe of Lecture III. In that universe, we had a number of perspectives, two of which never had any entity in common, but often contained entities which could be sufficiently correlated to be regarded as belonging to the same thing. We will call one of these an " actual " private world when there is an actual spectator to which it appears, and " ideal " when it is merely constructed on principles of continuity. A physical thing consists, at each instant, of the whole set of its aspects at that instant, in all the different worlds ; thus a momentary state of a thing is a whole set of aspects. An " ideal " appearance will be an aspect merely calculated, but not actually perceived by any spectator. An " ideal " state of a thing will be a state at a moment when all its appearances are ideal. An ideal thing will be one whose states at all times are ideal. Ideal appearances, states, and things, since they are calculated, must be functions of actual appearances, states, and things ; in fact, ultimately, they must be functions of actual appearances. Thus it is unnecessary, for the enunciation of the laws of physics, to assign any reality to ideal elements : it is enough to accept them as logical constructions, provided we have means of knowing how to determine when they become actual. This, in fact, we have with some degree of approximation ; the starry heaven, for instance, becomes actual whenever we choose to look at it. It is open to us to believe that the ideal elements exist, and there can be no reason for *dis*believing this ; but unless in virtue of some *a priori* law we cannot *know* it, for empirical knowledge is confined to what we actually observe.

We come now to the conception of space. Here it is of the greatest importance to distinguish sharply between the space of physics and the space of one man's experience. It is the latter that must concern us first.

People who have never read any psychology seldom realize how much mental labour has gone into the construction of the one all-embracing space into which all sensible objects are supposed to fit. Kant, who was unusually ignorant of psychology, described space as " an infinite given whole," whereas a moment's psychological reflection shows that a space which is infinite is not given, while a space which can be called given is not infinite. What the nature of " given " space really is, is a difficult question, upon which psychologists are by no means agreed. But some general remarks may be made, which will suffice to show the problems, without taking sides on any psychological issue still in debate.

The first thing to notice is that different senses have different spaces. The space of sight is quite different from the space of touch : it is only by experience in infancy that we learn to correlate them. In later life, when we see an object within reach, we know how to touch it, and more or less what it will feel like ; if we touch an object with our eyes shut, we know where we should have to look for it, and more or less what it would look like. But this knowledge is derived from early experience of the correlation of certain kinds of touch-sensations with certain kinds of sight-sensations. The one space into which both kinds of sensations fit is an intellectual construction, not a datum. And besides touch and sight, there are other kinds of sensation which give other, though less important spaces : these also have to be fitted into the one space by means of experienced correlations. And as in the case of things, so here : the one all-embracing space, though convenient as a way of speaking, need not be supposed really to exist. All that experience makes certain is the several spaces of the several senses correlated by empirically discovered laws. The one space may turn out to be valid as a logical construction, compounded of the several spaces, but there is no good reason to assume its independent metaphysical reality.

Another respect in which the spaces of immediate experience differ from the space of geometry and physics is in regard to *points*, The space of geometry *and* physics consists of an infinite number of points, but no one has ever seen or touched a point. If there are points in a sensible space, they must be an inference. It is not easy to see any way in which, as independent entities, they could be validly inferred from the data ; thus here again, we shall have, if possible, to find some logical construction, some complex assemblage of immediately given objects, which will have the geometrical properties required of points. It is customary to think of points as simple and infinitely small, but geometry in no way demands that we should think of them in this way. All that is necessary for geometry is that they should have mutual relations possessing certain enumerated abstract properties, and it may be that an assemblage of data of sensation will serve this purpose. Exactly how this is to be done I do not yet know, but it seems fairly certain that it can be done.

An illustrative method, simplified so as to be easily manipulated, has been invented by Dr. Whitehead for the purpose of showing how points might be manufactured from sense-data together with other structurally analogous particulars. This method is set forth in his *Principles of Natural Knowledge* (Cambridge, 1919) and *Concept of Nature* (Cambridge, 1920). It is impossible to explain this method more concisely than in those books, to which the reader is therefore referred. But a few words may be said by way of explaining the general principles underlying the method. We have first of all to observe that there are no infinitesimal sense-data : any surface we can see, for example, must be of some finite extent. We assume that this applies, not only to sense-data, but to the whole of the stuff composing the world : whatever is not an abstraction has some finite spatio-temporal size, though we cannot discover a lower limit to the sizes that are possible. But what appears as one undivided whole is often found, under the influence of attention, to split up into parts contained within the whole. Thus one spatial datum may be contained within another, and entirely enclosed by the other. This relation of enclosure, by the help of some very natural hypotheses, will enable us to define a " point " as a certain set of spatial objects ; roughly speaking, the set will consist of all volumes which would naturally be said to contain the point.

It should be observed that Dr. Whitehead's abstract logical methods are applicable equally to psychological space, physical space, time, and space-time. But as applied to psychological space, they do not yield continuity unless we assume that sense-data always contain parts which are not sense-data. Sense-data have a minimum size, below which nothing is experienced ; but Dr. Whitehead's methods postulate that there shall be no such minimum. We cannot therefore construct a continuum without assuming the existence of particulars which are not experienced. This, however, does not constitute a real difficulty, since there is no reason to suppose that the space of our immediate experience possesses mathematical continuity. The full employment of Dr. Whitehead's methods, therefore, belongs rather to physical space than to the space of experience. This question will concern us again later, when we come to consider physical space-time and its partial correlation with the space and time of experience.

A very interesting attempt to show the kinds of geometry that can be constructed out of the actual materials supplied in sensation will be found in Jean Nicod's *La géométrie dans le monde sensible* (Paris, 1923).

The question of time, so long as we confine ourselves to one private world, is rather less complicated than that of space, and we can see pretty clearly how it might be dealt with by such methods as we have been considering. Events of which we are conscious do not last merely for a mathematical instant, but always for some finite time, however short. Even if there be a physical world such as the mathematical theory of motion supposes, impressions on our sense-organs produce sensations which are not merely and strictly instantaneous, and therefore the objects of sense of which we are immediately conscious are not strictly instantaneous. Instants, therefore, are not among the data of experience, and, if legitimate, must be either inferred or constructed. It is difficult to see how they can be validly inferred ; thus we are left with the alternative that they must be constructed. How is this to be done ?

Immediate experience provides us with two time-relations among events : they may be simultaneous, or one may be earlier and the other later. These two are both part of the crude data ; it is not the case that only the events are given, and their time-order is added by our subjective activity. The time-order, within certain limits, is as much given as the events. In any story of adventure you will find such passages as the following : " With a cynical smile he pointed the revolver at the breast of the dauntless youth. ' At the word *three* I shall fire,' he said. The words one and two had already been spoken with a cool and deliberate distinctness. The word *three* was forming on his lips. At this moment a blinding flash of lightning rent the air." Here we have simultaneity—not due, as Kant would have us believe, to the subjective mental apparatus of the dauntless youth, but given as objectively as the revolver and the lightning. And it is equally given in immediate experience that the words *one* and *two* come earlier than the flash. These time-relations hold between events which are not strictly instantaneous. Thus one event may begin sooner than another, and therefore be before it, but may continue after the other has begun, and therefore be also simultaneous with it. If it persists after the other is over, it will also be later than the other. Earlier, simultaneous, and later, are not inconsistent with each other when we are concerned with events which last for a finite time, however short ; they only become inconsistent when we are dealing with something instantaneous.

It is to be observed that we cannot give what may be called *absolute* dates, but only dates determined by events. We cannot point to a time itself, but only to some event occurring at that time. There is therefore no reason in experience to suppose that there are times as opposed to events : the events, ordered by the relations of simultaneity and succession, are all that experience provides. Hence, unless we are to introduce superfluous metaphysical entities, we must, in defining what we can regard as an instant, proceed by means of some construction which assumes nothing beyond events and their temporal relations.

If we wish to assign a date exactly by means of events, how shall we proceed ? If we take any one event, we cannot assign our date exactly, because the event is not instantaneous, that is to say, it may be simultaneous with two events which are not simultaneous with each other. In order to assign a date exactly, we must be able, theoretically, to determine whether any given event is before, at, or after this date, and we must know that any other date is either before or after this date, but not simultaneous with it. Suppose, now, instead of taking one event A, we take two events A and B, and suppose A and B partly overlap, but B ends before A ends. Then an event which is simultaneous with both A and B must exist during the time when A and B overlap ; thus we have come rather nearer to a precise date than when we considered A and B alone. Let C be an event which is simultaneous with both A and B, but which ends before either A or B has ended. Then an event which is simultaneous with A and B and C must exist during

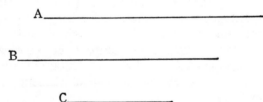

the time when all three overlap, which is a still shorter time. Proceeding in this way, by taking more and more events, a new event which is dated as simultaneous with all of them becomes gradually more and more accurately dated. This suggests a way by which a completely accurate date can be defined.

Let us take a group of events of which any two overlap, so that there is some time, however short, when they all exist. If there is any other event which is simultaneous with all of these, let us add it to the group ; let us go on until we have constructed a group such that no event outside the group is simultaneous with all of them, but all the events inside the group are simultaneous with each other. Let us define this whole group as an instant of time. It remains to show that it has the properties we expect of an instant.

What are the properties we expect of instants ? First, they must form a series : of any two, one must be before the other, and the other must be not before the one ; if one is before another, and the other before a third, the first must be before the third. Secondly, every event must be at a certain number of instants ; two events are simultaneous if they are at the same instant, and one is before the other if there is an instant, at which the one is, which is earlier than some instant at which the other is. Thirdly, if we assume that there is always some change going on somewhere during the time when any given event persists, the series of instants ought to be compact, i.e. given any two instants, there ought to be other instants between them. Do instants, as we have defined them, have these properties ?

We shall say that an event is " at " an instant when it is a member of the group by which the instant is constituted ; and we shall say that one instant is before another if the group which is the one instant contains an event which is earlier than, but not simultaneous with, some event in the group which is the other instant. When one event is earlier than, but not simultaneous with another, we shall say that it "wholly precedes" the other. Now we know that of two events which belong to one experience but are not simultaneous, there must be one which wholly precedes the other, and in that case the other cannot also wholly precede the one ; we also know that, if one event wholly precedes another, and the other wholly precedes a third, then the first wholly precedes the third. From these facts it is easy to deduce that the instants as we have defined them form a series.

We have next to show that every event is "at" least one instant, i.e. that, given any event, there is at least one class, such as we used in defining instants, of which it is a member. For this purpose, consider all the events which are simultaneous with a given event, and do not begin later, i.e. are not wholly after anything simultaneous with it. We will call these the "initial contemporaries of the given event. It will be found that this class of events is the first instant at which the given event exists, provided every event wholly after some contemporary of the given event is wholly after some *initial* contemporary of it.

Finally, the series of instants will be compact if, given any two events of which one wholly precedes the other, there are events wholly after the one and simultaneous with something wholly before the other. Whether this is the case or not, is an empirical question ; but if it is not, there is no reason to expect the time-series to be compact.[1]

[1] The assumptions made concerning time-relations in one experience in the above are as follows :—

I. In order to secure that instants form a series, we assume :

Thus our definition of instants secures all that mathematics requires, without having to assume the existence of any disputable metaphysical entities.

With regard to compactness in the time of one experience, there are the same observations to make as in the case of space. The events which we experience have not only a finite duration, but a duration which cannot sink below a certain minimum ; therefore they will only fit into a *compact* series if we either bring in events wholly outside our experience, or assume that experienced events have parts which we do not experience, or postulate that we can experi-

(a) No event wholly precedes itself. (An " event " is defined as whatever is simultaneous with something or other.)

(b) If one event wholly precedes another, and the other wholly precedes a third, then the first wholly precedes the third.

(c) If one event wholly precedes another, it is not simultaneous with it.

(d) Of two events which are not simultaneous, one must wholly precede the other.

II. In order to secure that the initial contemporaries of a given event should form an instant, we assume :

(e) An event wholly after some contemporary of a given event is wholly after some *initial* contemporary of the given event.

III. In order to secure that the series of instants shall be compact, we assume :

(f) If one event wholly precedes another, there is an event wholly after the one and simultaneous with something wholly before the other.

This assumption entails the consequence that if one event covers the whole of a stretch of time immediately preceding another event, then it must have at least one instant in common with the other event ; i.e. it is impossible for one event to cease just before another begins. I do not know whether this should be regarded as inadmissible. For a mathematico-logical treatment of the above topics, cf. N. Wiener, " A Contribution to the Theory of Relative Position," *Proc. Camb. Phil. Soc.*, xvii. 5, pp. 441–449.

ence an infinite number of events at once. Here, again, the full application of our logico-mathematical method is only possible when we come to physical time. This topic will be discussed again near the end of Lecture V.

Instants may also be defined by means of the enclosure-relation, exactly as was done in the case of points. One object will be temporally enclosed by another when it is simultaneous with the other, but not before or after it. Whatever encloses temporally or is enclosed temporally we shall call an " event." In order that the relation of temporal enclosure may lead to instants we require (1) that it should be transitive, i.e. that if one event encloses another, and the other a third, then the first encloses the third ; (2) that every event encloses itself, but if one event encloses another different event, then the other does not enclose the one ; (3) that given any set of events such that there is at least one event enclosed by all of them, then there is an event enclosing all that they all enclose, and itself enclosed by all of them ; (4) that there is at least one event. To ensure infinite divisibility, we require also that every event should enclose events other than itself. Assuming these characteristics, temporal enclosure can be made to give rise to a compact series of instants. We can now form an " enclosure-series " of events, by choosing a group of events such that of any two there is one which encloses the other ; this will be a " punctual enclosure-series " if, given any other enclosure-series such that every member of our first series encloses some member of our second, then every member of our second series encloses some member of our first. Then an " instant " is the class of all events which enclose members of a given punctual enclosure-series.

The correlation of the times of different private worlds is a more difficult matter. We saw, in Lecture III, that different private worlds often contain correlated appearances, such as common sense would regard as appearances of the same " thing." When two appearances in different worlds are so correlated as to belong to one momentary " state " of a thing, it would be natural to regard them as simultaneous, and as thus affording a simple means of correlating different private times. But this can only be regarded as a first approximation. What we call one sound will be heard sooner by people near the source of the sound than by people further from it, and the same applies, though in a less degree, to light. Thus two correlated appearances in different worlds are not necessarily to be regarded as occurring at the same date in physical time, though they will be parts of one momentary state of a thing. The correlation of different private times is regulated by the desire to secure the simplest possible statement of the laws of physics, and thus raises rather complicated technical problems ; these problems are dealt with by the theory of relativity, and show that it is impossible validly to construct one all-embracing time having any physical significance.

The above brief outline must not be regarded as more than tentative and suggestive. It is intended merely to show the kind of way in which, given a world with the kind of properties that psychologists find in the world of sense, it may be possible, by means of purely logical constructions, to make it amenable to mathematical treatment by defining series or classes of sense-data which can be called respectively particles, points, and instants. If such constructions are possible, then mathematical physics is applicable to the real world, in spite of the fact that its particles, points, and instants are not to be found among actually existing entities.

The space-time of physics has not a very close relation to the space and time of the world of one person's experience. Everything that occurs in one person's experience must, from the standpoint of physics, be located within that person's body ; this is evident from considerations of causal continuity. What occurs when I see a star occurs as the result of light-waves impinging on the retina, and causing a process in the optic nerve and brain ; therefore the occurrence called " seeing a star " must be in the brain. If we define a piece of matter as a set of events (as was suggested above), the sensation of seeing a star will be one of the events which *are* the brain of the percipient at the time of the perception. Thus every event that I experience will be one of the events which constitute some part of my body. The space of (say) my visual perceptions is only *correlated* with physical space, more or less approximately ; from the physical point of view, whatever I see is inside my head. I do not see physical objects ; I see effects which they produce in the region where my brain is. The correlation of visual and physical space is rendered approximate by the fact that my visual sensations are not *wholly* due each to some physical object, but also partly to the intervening medium. Further, the relation of visual sensation to physical object is one-many, not not-one, because our senses are more or less vague : things which look different under the microscope may be indistinguishable to the naked eye. The inferences from perceptions to physical facts depend always upon causal laws, which enable us to bring past history to bear ; e.g. if we have just examined an object under a microscope, we assume that it is still very similar to what we then saw it to be, or rather, to what we inferred it to be from what we then saw. It is through history and testimony, together with causal laws, that we arrive at physical knowledge which is much more precise than anything inferable from the perceptions of one moment. History, testimony, and causal laws are, of course, in their various degrees, open to question. But we are not now considering whether physics is true, but how, if it is true, its world is related to that of the senses.

With regard to time, the relation of psychology to physics is surprisingly simple. The time of our experience is the time which results, in physics, from taking our own body as the origin. Seeing that all the events in my experience are, for physics, in my body, the time-interval between them is what relativity theory calls the " interval " (in space-time) between them. Thus the time-interval between two events in one person's experience retains a direct physical significance in the theory of relativity. But the merging of physical space and time into space-time does not correspond to anything in psychology. Two events which are simultaneous in my experience may be spatially separate in psychical space, e.g. when I see two stars at once. But in physical space these two events are not separated, and indeed they occur in the same place in space-time. Thus in this respect relativity theory has complicated the relation between perception and physics.

The problem which the above considerations are intended to elucidate is one whose importance and even existence has been concealed by the unfortunate separation of different studies which prevails throughout the civilized world. Physicists, ignorant and contemptuous of philosophy, have been content to assume their particles, points, and instants in practice, while conceding, with ironical politeness, that their concepts laid no claim to metaphysical validity. Metaphysicians, obsessed by the idealistic opinion that only mind is real, and the Parmenidean belief that the real is unchanging, repeated one after another the supposed contradictions in the notions of matter, space, and time, and therefore naturally made no endeavour to invent a tenable theory of particles, points, and instants. Psychologists, who have done invaluable work in bringing to light the chaotic nature of the crude materials supplied by unmanipulated sensation, have been ignorant of mathematics and modern logic, and have therefore been content to say that matter, space, and time are "intellectual constructions," without making any attempt to show in detail either how the intellect can construct them, or what secures the practical validity which physics shows them to possess. Philosophers, it is to be hoped, will come to recognize that they cannot achieve any solid success in such problems without some slight knowledge of logic, mathematics, and physics; meanwhile, for want of students with the necessary equipment, this vital problem remains unattempted and unknown.[1]

There are, it is true, two authors, both physicists, who have done something, though not much, to bring about a recognition of the problem as one demanding study. These two authors are Poincaré and Mach, Poincaré especially in his *Science and Hypothesis*,

[1] This was written in 1914. Since then, largely as a result of the general theory of relativity, a great deal of valuable work has been done; I should wish to mention specially Professor Eddington, Dr. Whitehead, and Dr. Broad, as having contributed, from different angles, to the solution of the problems dealt with in this lecture.

Mach especially in his *Analysis of Sensations*. Both of them, however, admirable as their work is, seem to me to suffer from a general philosophical bias. Poincaré is Kantian, while Mach is ultra-empiricist ; with Poincaré almost all the mathematical part of physics is merely conventional, while with Mach the sensation as a mental event is identified with its object as a part of the physical world. Nevertheless, both these authors, and especially Mach, deserve mention as having made serious contributions to the consideration of our problem.

When a point or an instant is defined as a class of sensible qualities, the first impression produced is likely to be one of wild and wilful paradox. Certain considerations apply here, however, which will again be relevant when we come to the definition of numbers. There is a whole type of problems which can be solved by such definitions, and almost always there will be at first an effect of paradox. Given a set of objects any two of which have a relation of the sort called " symmetrical and transitive," it is almost certain that we shall come to regard them as all having some common quality, or as all having the same relation to some one object outside the set. This kind of case is important, and I shall therefore try to make it clear even at the cost of some repetition of previous definitions.

A relation is said to be " symmetrical " when, if one term has this relation to another, then the other also has it to the one. Thus " brother or sister " is a " symmetrical " relation : if one person is a brother or a sister of another, then the other is a brother or sister of the one. Simultaneity, again, is a symmetrical relation ; so is equality in size. A relation is said to be " transitive " when, if one term has this relation to another, and the other to a third, then the one has it to the third. The symmetrical relations mentioned just now are also transitive—provided, in the case of " brother or sister," we allow a person to be counted as his or her own brother or sister, and provided, in the case of simultaneity, we mean complete simultaneity, i.e. beginning and ending together.

But many relations are transitive without being symmetrical—for instance, such relations as " greater," " earlier," " to the right of," " ancestor of," in fact all such relations as give rise to series. Other relations are symmetrical without being transitive—for example, difference in any respect. If A is of a different age from B, and B of a different age from C, it does not follow that A is of a different age from C. Simultaneity, again, in the case of events which last for a finite time, will not necessarily be transitive if it only means that the times of the two events overlap. If A ends just after B has begun, and B ends just after C has begun, A and B will be simultaneous in this sense, and so will B and C, but A and C may well not be simultaneous.

All the relations which can naturally be represented as equality in any respect, or as possession of a common property, are transitive and symmetrical—this applies, for example, to such relations as being of the same height or weight or colour. Owing to the fact that possession of a common property gives rise to a transitive symmetrical relation, we come to imagine that wherever such a relation occurs it must be due to a common property. " Being equally numerous " is a transitive symmetrical relation of two collections ; hence we imagine that both have a common property, called their number. " Existing at a given instant " (in the sense in which we defined an instant) is a transitive symmetrical relation ; hence we come to think that there really is an instant which confers a common property on all the things existing at that instant. " Being states of a given thing " is a transitive symmetrical relation ; hence we come to imagine that there really is a thing, other than the series of states, which accounts for the transitive symmetrical relation. In all such cases, the class of terms that have the given transitive symmetrical relation to a given term will fulfil all the formal requisites of a common property of all the members of the class. Since there certainly is the class, while any other common property may be illusory, it is prudent, in order to avoid needless assumptions, to substitute the class for the common property which would be ordinarily assumed. This is the reason for the definitions we have adopted, and this is the source of the apparent paradoxes. No harm is done if there are such common properties as language assumes, since we do not deny them, but merely abstain from asserting them. But if there are not such common properties in any given case, then our method has secured us against error. In the absence of special knowledge, therefore, the method we have adopted is the only one which is safe, and which avoids the risk of introducing fictitious metaphysical entities.

LECTURE V

THE THEORY OF CONTINUITY

THE theory of continuity, with which we shall be occupied in the present lecture, is, in most of its refinements and developments, a purely mathematical subject—very beautiful, very important, and very delightful, but not, strictly speaking, a part of philosophy. The logical basis of the theory alone belongs to philosophy, and alone will occupy us to-night. The way the problem of continuity enters into philosophy is, broadly speaking, the following : Space and time are treated by mathematicians as consisting of points and instants, but they also have a property, easier to feel than to define, which is called continuity, and is thought by many philosophers to be destroyed when they are resolved into points and instants. Zeno, as we shall see, proved that analysis into points and instants was impossible if we adhered to the view that the number of points or instants in a finite space or time must be finite. Later philosophers, believing infinite number to be self-contradictory, have found here an antinomy : Spaces and times could not consist of a *finite* number of points and instants, for such reasons as Zeno's ; they could not consist of an *infinite* number of points and instants, because infinite numbers were supposed to be self-contradictory. Therefore spaces and times, if real at all, must not be regarded as composed of points and instants.

But even when points and instants, as independent entities, are discarded, as they were by the theory advocated in our last lecture, the problems of continuity, as I shall try to show presently, remain, in a practically unchanged form. Let us therefore, to begin with, admit points and instants, and consider the problems in connection with this simpler or at least more familiar hypothesis.

The argument against continuity, in so far as it rests upon the supposed difficulties of infinite numbers, has been disposed of by the positive theory of the infinite, which will be considered in Lecture VII. But there remains a feeling—of the kind that led Zeno to the contention that the arrow in its flight is at rest—which suggests that points and instants, even if they are infinitely numerous, can only give a jerky motion, a succession of different immobilities, not the smooth transitions with which the senses have made us familiar. This feeling is due, I believe, to a failure to realize imaginatively, as well as abstractly, the nature of continuous series as they appear in mathematics. When a theory has been apprehended logically, there is often a long and serious labour still required in order to *feel* it : it is necessary to dwell upon it, to thrust out from the mind, one by one, the misleading suggestions of false but more familiar theories, to acquire the kind of intimacy which, in the case of a foreign language, would enable us to think and dream in it, not merely to construct laborious sentences by the help of grammar and dictionary. It is, I believe, the absence of this kind of intimacy which makes many philosophers regard the mathematical doctrine of continuity as an inadequate explanation of the continuity which we experience in the world of sense.

In the present lecture, I shall first try to explain in outline what the mathematical theory of continuity is in its philosophically important essentials. The application to actual space and time will not be in question to begin with. I do not see any reason to suppose that the points and instants which mathematicians introduce in dealing with space and time are actual physically existing entities, but I do see reason to suppose that the continuity of actual space and time may be more or less analogous to mathematical continuity. The theory of mathematical continuity is an abstract logical theory, not dependent for its validity upon any properties of actual space and time. What is claimed for it is that, when it is understood, certain characteristics of space and time, previously very hard to analyse, are found not to present any logical difficulty. What we know empirically about space and time is insufficient to enable us to decide between various mathematically possible alternatives, but these alternatives are all fully intelligible and fully adequate to the observed facts. For the present, however, it will be well to forget space and time and the continuity of sensible change, in order to return to these topics equipped with the weapons provided by the abstract theory of continuity.

Continuity, in mathematics, is a property only possible to a *series* of terms, i.e. to terms arranged in an order, so that we can say of any two that one comes *before* the other. Numbers in order of magnitude, the points on a line from left to right, the moments of time from earlier to later, are instances of series. The notion of order, which is here introduced, is one which is not required in the theory of cardinal number. It is possible to know that two classes have the same number of terms without knowing any order in which they are to be taken. We have an instance of this in such a case as English husbands and English wives : we can see that there must be the same number of husbands as of wives, without having to arrange them in a series. But continuity, which we are now to consider, is essentially a property of an order : it does not belong to a set of terms in themselves, but only to a set in a certain order. A set of terms which can be arranged in one order can always also be arranged in other orders, and a set of terms which can be arranged in a continuous order can always be arranged in orders which are not continuous. Thus the essence of continuity must not be sought in the nature of the set of terms, but in the nature of their arrangement in a series.

Mathematicians have distinguished different degrees of continuity, and have confined the word " continuous," for technical purposes, to series having a certain high degree of continuity. But for philosophical purposes, all that is important in continuity is introduced by the lowest degree of continuity, which is called " compactness." A series is called " compact " when no two terms are consecutive, but between any two there are others. One of the simplest examples of a compact series is the series of fractions in order of magnitude. Given any two fractions, however near together, there are other fractions greater than the one and smaller than the other, and therefore no two fractions are consecutive. There is no fraction, for example, which is next after $\frac{1}{2}$: if we choose some fraction which is very little greater than $\frac{1}{2}$, say $\frac{51}{100}$, we can find others, such as $\frac{101}{200}$, which are nearer to $\frac{1}{2}$. Thus between any two fractions, however little they differ, there are an infinite number of other fractions. Mathematical space and time also have this property of compactness, though whether actual space and time have it is a further question, dependent upon empirical evidence, and probably incapable of being answered with certainty.

In the case of abstract objects such as fractions, it is perhaps not very difficult to realize the logical possibility of their forming a compact series. The difficulties that might be felt are those of infinity, for in a compact series the number of terms between any two given terms must be infinite. But when these difficulties have been solved, the mere compactness in itself offers no great obstacle to the imagination. In more concrete cases, however, such as motion, compactness becomes much more repugnant to our habits of thought. It will therefore be desirable to consider explicitly the mathematical account of motion, with a view to making its logical possibility felt. The mathematical account of motion is perhaps artificially simplified when regarded as describing what actually occurs in the physical world ; but what actually occurs must be capable, by a certain amount of logical manipulation, of being brought within the scope of the mathematical account, and must, in its analysis, raise just such problems as are raised in their simplest form by this account. Neglecting, therefore, for the present, the question of its physical adequacy, let us devote ourselves merely to considering its possibility as a formal statement of the nature of motion.

In order to simplify our problem as much as possible, let us imagine a tiny speck of light moving along a scale. What do we mean by saying that the motion is continuous ? It is not necessary for our purposes to consider the whole of what the mathematician means by this statement : only part of what he means is philosophically important. One part of what he means is that, if we consider any two positions of the speck occupied at any two instants, there will be other intermediate positions occupied at intermediate instants. However near together we take the two positions, the speck will not jump suddenly from the one to the other, but will pass through an infinite number of other positions on the way. Every distance, however small, is traversed by passing through all the infinite series of positions between the two ends of the distance.

But at this point imagination suggests that we may describe the continuity of motion by saying that the speck always passes from one position at one instant to *the next* position at *the next* instant. As soon as we say this or imagine it, we fall into error, because there is no *next* point or *next* instant. If there were, we should find Zeno's paradoxes, in some form, unavoidable, as will appear in our next lecture. One simple paradox may serve as an illustration. If our speck is in motion along the scale throughout the whole of a certain time, it cannot be at the same point at two consecutive instants. But it cannot, from one instant to the next, travel further than from one point to the next, for if it did, there would be no instant at which it was in the positions intermediate between that at the first instant and that at the next, and we agreed that the continuity of motion excludes the possibility of such sudden jumps. It follows that our speck must, so long as it moves, pass from one point at one instant to the next point at the next instant. Thus there will be just one perfectly definite velocity with which all motions must take place : no motion can be faster than this, and no motion can be slower. Since this conclusion is false, we must reject the hypothesis upon which it is based, namely that there are consecutive points and instants.[1] Hence the continuity of motion must not be supposed to consist in a body's occupying consecutive positions at consecutive times.

The difficulty to imagination lies chiefly, I think, in keeping out the suggestion of *infinitesimal* distances and times. Suppose we halve a given distance, and then halve the half, and so on, we can continue the process as long as we please, and the longer we continue it, the smaller the resulting distance becomes. This infinite divisibility seems, at first sight, to imply that there are infinitesimal distances, i.e. distances so small that any finite fraction of an inch would be greater. This, however, is an error. The continued bisection of our distance, though it gives us continually smaller distances, gives us always *finite* distances. If our original distance was an inch, we reach successively half an inch, a quarter of an inch, an eighth, a sixteenth, and so on ; but every one of this infinite series of diminishing distances is finite. " But," it may be said, " *in the end* the distance will grow infinitesimal." No, because there is no end. The process of bisection is one which can, theoretically, be carried on for ever, without any last term being attained. Thus infinite divisibility of distances, which must be admitted, does not imply that there are distances so small that any finite distance would be larger.

It is easy, in this kind of question, to fall into an elementary logical blunder. Given any finite distance, we can find a smaller distance ; this may be expressed in the ambiguous form " there is a distance smaller than any finite distance." But if this is then

---

[1] The above paradox is essentially the same as Zeno's argument of the stadium which will be considered in our next lecture.

interpreted as meaning " there is a distance such that, whatever finite distance may be chosen, the distance in question is smaller," then the statement is false. Common language is ill adapted to expressing matters of this kind, and philosophers who have been dependent on it have frequently been misled by it.

In a continuous motion, then, we shall say that at any given instant the moving body occupies a certain position, and at other instants it occupies other positions ; the interval between any two instants and between any two positions is always finite, but the continuity of the motion is shown in the fact that, however near together we take the two positions and the two instants, there are an infinite number of positions still nearer together, which are occupied at instants that are also still nearer together. The moving body never jumps from one position to another, but always passes by a gradual transition through an infinite number of intermediaries. At a given instant, it is where it is, like Zeno's arrow ; [1] but we cannot say that it is at rest at the instant, since the instant does not last for a finite time, and there is not a beginning and end of the instant with an interval between them. Rest consists in being in the same position at all the instants throughout a certain finite period, however short ; it does not consist simply in a body's being where it is at a given instant. This whole theory, as is obvious, depends upon the nature of compact series, and demands, for its full comprehension, that compact series should have become familiar and easy to the imagination as well as to deliberate thought.

What is required may be expressed in mathematical language by saying that the position of a moving body must be a continuous function of the time. To define

[1] See next lecture.

accurately what this means, we proceed as follows. Consider a particle which, at the moment t, is at the

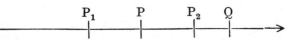

point P. Choose now any small portion $P_1 P_2$ of the path of the particle, this portion being one which contains P. We say then that, if the motion of the particle is continuous at the time t, it must be possible to find two instants t_1, t_2, one earlier than t and one later, such that throughout the whole time from t_1 to t_2 (both included), the particle lies between P_1 and P_2. And we say that this must still hold however small we make the portion $P_1 P_2$. When this is the case, we say that the motion is continuous at the time t ; and when the motion is continuous at all times, we say that the motion as a whole is continuous. It is obvious that if the particle were to jump suddenly from P to some other point Q, our definition would fail for all intervals $P_1 P_2$ which were too small to include Q. Thus our definition affords an analysis of the continuity of motion, while admitting points and instants and denying infinitesimal distances in space or periods in time.

Philosophers, mostly in ignorance of the mathematician's analysis, have adopted other and more heroic methods of dealing with the *prima facie* difficulties of continuous motion. A typical and recent example of philosophic theories of motion is afforded by Bergson, whose views on this subject I have examined elsewhere.[1]

Apart from definite arguments, there are certain feelings, rather than reasons, which stand in the way of an acceptance of the mathematical account of

[1] *Monist*, July 1912, pp. 337–341.

motion. To begin with, if a body is moving at all
fast, we *see* its motion just as we see its colour. A
slow motion, like that of the hour-hand of a watch,
is only known in the way which mathematics would
lead us to expect, namely by observing a change of
position after a lapse of time ; but, when we observe
the motion of the second-hand, we do not merely
see first one position and then another—we see something as directly sensible as colour. What is this
something that we see, and that we call visible motion ?
Whatever it is, it is *not* the successive occupation of
successive positions : something beyond the mathematical theory of motion is required to account for it.
Opponents of the mathematical theory emphasize this
fact. " Your theory," they say, " may be very
logical, and might apply admirably to some other
world ; but in this actual world, actual motions are
quite different from what your theory would declare
them to be, and require, therefore, some different
philosophy from yours for their adequate explanation."

The objection thus raised is one which I have no
wish to underrate, but I believe it can be fully answered
without departing from the methods and the outlook
which have led to the mathematical theory of motion.
Let us, however, first try to state the objection more
fully.

If the mathematical theory is adequate, nothing
happens when a body moves except that it is in different
places at different times. But in this sense the hour-
hand and the second-hand are equally in motion, yet
in the second-hand there is something perceptible to
our senses which is absent in the hour-hand. We can
see, at each moment, that the second-hand *is moving*,
which is different from seeing it first in one place and
then in another. This seems to involve our seeing

it simultaneously in a number of places, although it must also involve our seeing that it is in some of these places earlier than in others. If, for example, I move my hand quickly from left to right, you seem to see the whole movement at once, in spite of the fact that you know it begins at the left and ends at the right. It is this kind of consideration, I think, which leads Bergson and many others to regard a movement as really one indivisible whole, not the series of separate states imagined by the mathematician.

To this objection there are three supplementary answers, physiological, psychological, and logical. We will consider them successively.

(1) The physiological answer merely shows that, if the physical world is what the mathmatician supposes, its sensible appearance may nevertheless be expected to be what it is. The aim of this answer is thus the modest one of showing that the mathematical account is not impossible as applied to the physical world ; it does not even attempt to show that this account is necessary, or that an analogous account applies in psychology.

When any nerve is stimulated, so as to cause a sensation, the sensation does not cease instantaneously with the cessation of the stimulus, but dies away in a short finite time. A flash of lightning, brief as it is to our sight, is briefer still as a physical phenomenon : we continue to see it for a few moments after the light-waves have ceased to strike the eye. Thus in the case of a physical motion, if it is sufficiently swift, we shall actually at one instant see the moving body throughout a finite portion of its course, and not only at the exact spot where it is at that instant. Sensations, however, as they die away, grow gradually

fainter ; tnus the sensation due to a stimulus which
is recently past is not exactly like the sensation due
to a present stimulus. It follows from this that,
when we see a rapid motion, we shall not only see a
number of positions of the moving body simultaneously,
but we shall see them with different degrees of intensity
—the present position most vividly, and the others
with diminishing vividness, until sensation fades
away into immediate memory. This state of things
accounts fully for the perception of motion. A motion
is *perceived*, not merely *inferred*, when it is sufficiently
swift for many positions to be sensible at one time ;
and the earlier and later parts of one perceived motion
are distinguished by the less and greater vividness of
the sensations.

This answer shows that physiology can account for
our perception of motion. But physiology, in speaking
of stimulus and sense-organs and a physical motion
distinct from the immediate object of sense, is assuming
the truth of physics, and is thus only capable of showing the physical account to be possible, not of showing
it to be *necessary*. This consideration brings us to
the psychological answer.

(2) The psychological answer to our difficulty about
motion is part of a vast theory, not yet worked out,
and only capable, at present, of being vaguely outlined.
We considered this theory in the third and fourth
lectures ; for the present, a mere sketch of its application to our present problem must suffice. The world of
physics, which was assumed in the physiological
answer, is obviously inferred from what is given in
sensation; yet as soon as we seriously consider what is
actually given in sensation, we find it apparently very
different from the world of physics. The question is
thus forced upon us : Is the inference from sense to

physics a valid one ? I believe the answer to be affirmative, for reasons which I suggested in the third and fourth lectures ; but the answer cannot be either short or easy. It consists, broadly speaking, in showing that, although the particles, points, and instants with which physics operates are not themselves given in experience, and are very likely not actually existing things, yet, out of the materials provided in sensation, together with other particulars structurally similar to these materials, it is possible to make logical constructions having the mathematical properties which physics assigns to particles, points, and instants. If this can be done, then all the propositions of physics can be translated, by a sort of dictionary, into propositions about the kinds of objects which are given in sensation.

Applying these general considerations to the case of motion, we find that, even within the sphere of immediate sense-data, it is necessary, or at any rate more consonant with the facts than any other equally simple view, to distinguish instantaneous states of objects, and to regard such states as forming a compact series. Let us consider a body which is moving swiftly enough for its motion to be perceptible, and long enough for its motion to be not wholly comprised in one sensation. Then, in spite of the fact that we see a finite extent of the motion at one instant, the extent which we see at one instant is different from that which we see at another. Thus we are brought back, after all, to a series of momentary views of the moving body, and this series will be compact, like the former physical series of points. In fact, though the *terms* of the series seem different, the mathematical character of the series is unchanged, and the whole mathematical theory of motion will apply to it *verbatim*.

When we are considering the actual data of sensation in this connection, it is important to realize that two sense-data may be, and *must* sometimes be, really different when we cannot perceive any difference between them. An old but conclusive reason for believing this was emphasized by Poincaré.[1] In all cases of sense-data capable of gradual change, we may find one sense-datum indistinguishable from another, and that other indistinguishable from a third, while yet the first and third are quite easily distinguishable. Suppose, for example, a person with his eyes shut is holding a weight in his hand, and someone noiselessly adds a small extra weight. If the extra weight is small enough, no difference will be perceived in the sensation. After a time, another small extra weight may be added, and still no change will be perceived ; but if both extra weights had been added at once, it may be that the change would be quite easily perceptible. Or, again, take shades of colour. It would be easy to find three stuffs of such closely similar shades that no difference could be perceived between the first and second, nor yet between the second and third, while yet the first and third would be distinguishable. In such a case, the second shade cannot be the same as the first, or it would be distinguishable from the third ; nor the same as the third, or it would be distinguishable from the first. It must, therefore, though indistinguishable from both, be really intermediate between them.

Such considerations as the above show that, although we cannot distinguish sense-data unless they differ by more than a certain amount, it is perfectly reasonable to suppose that sense-data of a given kind, such

[1] " Le continu mathématique," *Revue de Métaphysique et de Morale*, vol. i. p. 29.

as weights or colours, really form a compact series. The objections which may be brought from a psychological point of view against the mathematical theory of motion are not, therefore, objections to this theory properly understood, but only to a quite unnecessary assumption of simplicity in the momentary object of sense. Of the immediate object of sense, in the case of a visible motion, we may say that at each instant it is in all the positions which remain sensible at that instant ; but this set of positions changes continuously from moment to moment, and is amenable to exactly the same mathematical treatment as if it were a mere point. When we assert that some mathematical account of phenomena is correct, all that we primarily assert is that *something* definable in terms of the crude phenomena satisfies our formulæ ; and in this sense the mathematical theory of motion is applicable to the data of sensation as well as to the supposed particles of abstract physics.

There are a number of distinct questions which are apt to be confused when the mathematical continuum is said to be inadequate to the facts of sense. We may state these, in order of diminishing generality, as follows :—

(*a*) Are series possessing mathematical continuity logically possible ?

(*b*) Assuming that they are possible logically, are they not impossible as applied to actual sense-data, because, among actual sense-data, there are no such fixed mutually external terms as are to be found, e.g. in the series of fractions ?

(*c*) Does not the assumption of points and instants make the whole mathematical account fictitious ?

(*d*) Finally, assuming that all these objections have been answered, is there, in actual empirical fact, any sufficient reason to believe the world of sense continuous ?

Let us consider these questions in succession.

(*a*) The question of the logical possibility of the mathematical continuum turns partly on the elementary misunderstandings we considered at the beginning of the present lecture, partly on the possibility of the mathematical infinite, which will occupy our next two lectures, and partly on the logical form of the answer to the Bergsonian objection which we stated a few minutes ago. I shall say no more on this topic at present, since it is desirable first to complete the psychological answer.

(*b*) The question whether sense data are composed of mutually external units is not one which can be decided by empirical evidence. It is often urged that, as a matter of immediate experience, the sensible flux is devoid of divisions, and is falsified by the dissections of the intellect. Now I have no wish to argue that this view is *contrary* to immediate experience : I wish only to maintain that it is essentially incapable of being *proved* by immediate experience. As we saw, there must be among sense-data differences so slight as to be imperceptible : the fact that sense-data are immediately given does not mean that their differences also *must* be immediately given (though they *may* be). Suppose, for example, a coloured surface on which the colour changes gradually—so gradually that the difference of colour in two very neighbouring portions is imperceptible, while the difference between more widely separated portions is quite noticeable. The effect produced, in such a case, will be precisely that of "interpenetration," of transition which is not a matter of discrete units. And since it tends to be supposed that the colours, being immediate data, must *appear* different if they *are* different, it seems easily to follow that "interpenetration" must be the ultimately right account. But this does not follow. It is unconsciously assumed, as a premiss for a *reductio ad absurdum* of the analytic view, that, if A and B are immediate data, and A differs from B, then the fact that they differ must also be an immediate datum. It is difficult to say how this assumption arose, but I think it is to be connected with the confusion between "acquaintance" and "knowledge about." Acquaintance, which is what we derive from sense, does not, theoretically at least, imply even the smallest "knowledge about," i.e. it does not imply knowledge of any proposition concerning the object with which we are acquainted. It is a mistake to speak as if acquaintance had degrees : there is merely acquaintance and non-acquaintance. When we speak of becoming "better acquainted," as for instance with a person, what we must mean is, becoming acquainted with more parts of a certain whole ; but the acquaintance with each part is either complete or non-existent. Thus it is a mistake to say that if we were perfectly acquainted with an object we should know all about it. "Knowledge about " is knowledge of propositions, which is not involved necessarily in acquaintance with the constituents of the propositions. To know that two shades of colour are different is knowledge about them ; hence acquaintance with the two shades does not in any way necessitate the knowledge that they are different.

From what has just been said it follows that the nature of sense-data cannot be validly used to prove

that they are not composed of mutually external
units. It may be admitted, on the other hand, that
nothing in their empirical character specially necessi-
tates the view that they are composed of mutually
external units. This view, if it is held, must be held
on logical, not on empirical grounds. I believe that
the logical grounds are adequate to the conclusion.
They rest, at bottom, upon the impossibility of explaining complexity without assuming constituents.
It is undeniable that the visual field, for example,
is complex ; and so far as I can see, there is always
self-contradiction in the theories which, while admitting
this complexity, attempt to deny that it results from
a combination of mutually external units. But to
pursue this topic would lead us too far from our theme,
and I shall therefore say no more about it at present.

(c) It is sometimes urged that the mathematical
account of motion is rendered fictitious by its assumption of points and instants. Now there are here two
different questions to be distinguished. There is the
question of absolute or relative space and time, and
there is the question whether what occupies space
and time must be composed of elements which have
no extension or duration. And each of these questions in turn may take two forms, namely : (α) is
the hypothesis *consistent* with the facts and with
logic ? (β) is it *necessitated* by the facts or by logic ?
I wish to answer, in each case, yes to the first form
of the question, and no to the second. But in any
case the mathematical account of motion will not be
fictitious, provided a right interpretation is given
to the words " point " and " instant." A few words
on each alternative will serve to make this clear.

Formally, mathematics adopts an absolute theory
of space and time, i.e. it assumes that, besides the

things which are in space and time, there are also
entities, called "points" and "instants," which
are occupied by things. This view, however, though
advocated by Newton, has long been regarded by
mathematicians as merely a convenient fiction. There
is, so far as I can see, no conceivable evidence either
for or against it. It is logically possible, and it is
consistent with the facts. But the facts are also
consistent with the denial of spatial and temporal
entities over and above things with spatial and temporal relations. Hence, in accordance with Occam's
razor, we shall do well to abstain from either assuming
or denying points and instants. This means, so far
as practical working out is concerned, that we adopt the
relational theory ; for in practice the refusal to assume
points and instants has the same effect as the denial
of them. But in strict theory the two are quite
different, since the denial introduces an element of
unverifiable dogma which is wholly absent when we
merely refrain from the assertion. Thus, although
we shall derive points and instants from things, we
shall leave the bare possibility open that they may
also have an independent existence as simple entities.

We come now to the question whether the things
in space and time are to be conceived as composed of
elements without extension or duration, i.e. of elements
which only occupy a point and an instant. Physics,
formally, assumes in its differential equations that
things consist of elements which occupy only a point
at each instant, but persist throughout time. For
reasons explained in Lecture IV, the persistence of
things through time is to be regarded as the
formal result of a logical construction, not as necessarily
implying any actual persistence. The same motives,
in fact, which lead to the division of things into point-

particles, ought presumably to lead to their division into instant-particles, so that the ultimate *formal* constituent of the matter in physics will be a point-instant-particle. But such objects, as well as the particles of physics, are not data. The same economy of hypothesis, which dictates the practical adoption of a relative rather than an absolute space and time, also dictates the practical adoption of material elements which have a finite extension and duration. Since, as we saw in Lecture IV, points and instants can be constructed as logical functions of such elements, the mathematical account of motion, in which a particle passes continuously through a continuous series of points, can be interpreted in a form which assumes only elements which agree with our actual data in having a finite extension and duration. Thus, so far as the use of points and instants is concerned, the mathematical account of motion can be freed from the charge of employing fictions.

(*d*) But we must now face the question : Is there, in actual empirical fact, any sufficient reason to believe the world of sense continuous ? The answer here must, I think, be in the negative. We may say that the hypothesis of continuity is perfectly consistent with the facts and with logic, and that it is technically simpler than any other tenable hypothesis. But since our powers of discrimination among very similar sensible objects are not infinitely precise, it is quite impossible to decide between different theories which only differ in regard to what is below the margin of discrimination. If, for example, a coloured surface which we see consists of a finite number of very small surfaces, and if a motion which we see consists, like a cinematograph, of a large finite number of successive positions, there will be nothing empirically discoverable to show that objects of sense are not continuous. In what is called *experienced* continuity, such as is said to be given in sense, there is a large negative element : absence of perception of difference occurs in cases which are *thought* to give perception of absence of difference. When, for example, we cannot distinguish a colour A from a colour B, nor a colour B from a colour C, but can distinguish A from C, the indistinguishability is a purely negative fact, namely, that we do not *perceive* a difference. Even in regard to immediate data, this is no reason for denying that there is a difference. Thus, if we see a coloured surface whose colour changes gradually, its sensible appearance if the change is continuous will be indistinguishable from what it would be if the change were by small finite jumps.   If this is true, as it seems to be, it follows that there can never be any empirical evidence to demonstrate that the sensible world is continuous, and not a collection of a very large finite number of elements of which each differs from its neighbour in a finite though very small degree.   The continuity of space and time, the infinite number of different shades in the spectrum, and so on, are all in the nature of unverifiable hypotheses —perfectly possible logically, perfectly consistent with the known facts, and simpler technically than any other tenable hypotheses, but not the sole hypotheses which are logically and empirically adequate.

If a relational theory of instants is constructed, in which an " instant " is defined as a group of events simultaneous with each other and not all simultaneous with any event outside the group, then if our resulting series of instants is to be compact, it must be possible, if x wholly precedes y, to find an event z, simultaneous with part of x, which wholly precedes some event

which wholly precedes y. Now this requires that the
number of events concerned should be infinite in any
finite period of time. If this is to be the case in the
world of one man's sense-data, and if each sense-
datum is to have not less than a certain finite temporal
extension, it will be necessary to assume that we always
have an infinite number of sense-data simultaneous
with any given sense-datum. Applying similar considerations to space, and assuming that sense-data
are to have not less than a certain spatial extension,
it will be necessary to suppose that an infinite number
of sense-data overlap spatially with any given sense-
datum. This hypothesis is possible, if we suppose a
single sense-datum, e.g. in sight, to be a finite surface,
enclosing other surfaces which are also single sense-
data. But there are difficulties in such a hypothesis,
and I do not think that these difficulties could be
successfully met. If they cannot, we must do one
of two things : either declare that the world of one
man's sense-data is not continuous, or else refuse to
admit that there is any lower limit to the duration
and extension of a single sense-datum. The latter
hypothesis seems untenable, so that we are apparently
forced to conclude that the space of sense-data is
not continuous ; but that does not prevent us from
admitting that sense-data have parts which are not
sense-data, and that the space of these parts may be
continuous. The logical analysis we have been considering provides the apparatus for dealing with the
various hypotheses, and the empirical decision between
them is a problem for the psychologist.

(3) We have now to consider the *logical* answer to the
alleged difficulties of the mathematical theory of
motion, or rather to the positive theory which is
urged on the other side. The view urged explicitly

by Bergson, and implied in the doctrines of many philosophers, is, that a motion is something indivisible, not validly analysable into a series of states.   This is part of a much more general doctrine, which holds that analysis always falsifies, because the parts of a complex whole are different, as combined in that whole, from what they would otherwise be.   It is very difficult to state this doctrine in any form which has a precise meaning.   Often arguments are used which have no bearing whatever upon the question.   It is urged, for example, that when a man becomes a father, his nature is altered by the new relation in which he finds himself, so that he is not strictly identical with the man who was previously not a father.   This may be true, but it is a causal psychological fact, not a logical fact.   The doctrine would require that a man who is a father cannot be strictly identical with a man who is a son, because he is modified in one way by the relation of fatherhood and in another by that of sonship.   In fact, we may give a precise statement of the doctrine we are combating in the form : *There can never be two facts concerning the same thing.*   A fact concerning a thing always is or involves a relation to one or more entities ; thus two facts concerning the same thing would involve two relations of the same thing.   But the doctrine in question holds that a thing is so modified by its relations that it cannot be the same in one relation as in another.   Hence, if this doctrine is true, there can never be more than one fact concerning any one thing.   I do not think the philosophers in question have realized that this is the precise statement of the view they advocate, because in this form the view is so contrary to plain truth that its falsehood is evident as soon as it is stated.   The discussion of this question, however, involves so many logical subtleties, and is so beset with difficulties, that I shall not pursue it further at present.

When once the above general doctrine is rejected, it is obvious that, where there is change, there must be a succession of states. There cannot be change—and motion is only a particular case of change—unless there is something different at one time from what there is at some other time. Change, therefore, must involve relations and complexity, and must demand analysis. So long as our analysis has only gone as far as other smaller changes, it is not complete; if it is to be complete, it must end with terms that are not changes, but are related by a relation of earlier and later. In the case of changes which appear continuous, such as motions, it seems to be impossible to find anything other than change so long as we deal with finite periods of time, however short. We are thus driven back, by the logical necessities of the case, to the conception of instants without duration, or at any rate without any duration which even the most delicate instruments can reveal. This conception, though it can be made to seem difficult, is really easier than any other that the facts allow. It is a kind of logical framework into which any tenable theory must fit—not necessarily itself the statement of the crude facts, but a form in which statements which are true of the crude facts can be made by a suitable interpretation. The direct consideration of the crude facts of the physical world has been undertaken in earlier lectures; in the present lecture, we have only been concerned to show that nothing in the crude facts is inconsistent with the mathematical doctrine of continuity, or demands a continuity of a radically different kind from that of mathematical motion.

THE PROBLEM OF INFINITY
CONSIDERED HISTORICALLY

IT will be remembered that, when we enumerated the
grounds upon which the reality of the sensible world
has been questioned, one of those mentioned was the
supposed impossibility of infinity and continuity. In
view of our earlier discussion of physics, it would seem
that no *conclusive* empirical evidence exists in favour
of infinity or continuity in objects of sense or in matter.
Nevertheless, the explanation which assumes infinity
and continuity remains incomparably easier and more
natural, from a scientific point of view, than any other,
and since Georg Cantor has shown that the supposed
contradictions are illusory, there is no longer any reason
to struggle after a finitist explanation of the world.

The supposed difficulties of continuity all have their
source in the fact that a continuous series must have
an infinite number of terms, and are in fact difficulties
concerning infinity. Hence, in freeing the infinite
from contradiction, we are at the same time showing
the logical possibility of continuity as assumed in
science.

The kind of way in which infinity has been used to
discredit the world of sense may be illustrated by
Kant's first two antinomies. In the first, the thesis
states : " The world has a beginning in time, and as

regards space is enclosed within limits"; the antithesis states: "The world has no beginning and no
limits in space, but is infinite in respect of both time
and space." Kant professes to prove both these
propositions, whereas, if what we have said on modern
logic has any truth, it must be impossible to prove
either. In order, however, to rescue the world of
sense, it is enough to destroy the proof of *one* of
the two. For our present purpose, it is the proof that
the world is *finite* that interests us. Kant's argument
as regards space here rests upon his argument as
regards time. We need therefore only examine the
argument as regards time. What he says is as follows:

"For let us assume that the world has no beginning
as regards time, so that up to every given instant an
eternity has elapsed, and therefore an infinite series of
successive states of the things in the world has passed
by. But the infinity of a series consists just in this,
that it can never be completed by successive synthesis. Therefore an infinite past world-series is
impossible, and accordingly a beginning of the world
is a necessary condition of its existence; which was
the first thing to be proved."

Many different criticisms might be passed on this
argument, but we will content ourselves with a bare
minimum. To begin with, it is a mistake to define
the infinity of a series as "impossibility of completion
by successive synthesis." The notion of infinity, as
we shall see in the next lecture, is primarily a property
of *classes*, and only derivatively applicable to series;
classes which are infinite are given all at once by the
defining property of their members, so that there is
no question of "completion" or of "successive synthesis." And the word "synthesis," by suggesting
the mental activity of synthesizing, introduces, more

or less surreptitiously, that reference to mind by which all Kant's philosophy was infected. In the second place, when Kant says that an infinite series can "never" be completed by successive synthesis, all that he has even conceivably a right to say is that it cannot be completed *in a finite time*. Thus what he really proves is, at most, that if the world had no beginning, it must have already existed for an infinite time. This, however, is a very poor conclusion, by no means suitable for his purposes. And with this result we might, if we chose, take leave of the first antinomy.

It is worth while, however, to consider how Kant came to make such an elementary blunder. What happened in his imagination was obviously something like this : Starting from the present and going backwards in time, we have, if the world had no beginning, an infinite series of events. As we see from the word "synthesis," he imagined a mind trying to grasp these successively, *in the reverse order* to that in which they had occurred, i.e. going from the present backwards. *This* series is obviously one which has no end. But the series of events up to the present has an end, since it ends with the present. Owing to the inveterate subjectivism of his mental habits, he failed to notice that he had reversed the sense of the series by substituting backward synthesis for forward happening, and thus he supposed that it was necessary to identify the mental series, which had no end, with the physical series, which had an end but no beginning. It was this mistake, I think, which, operating unconsciously, led him to attribute validity to a singularly flimsy piece of fallacious reasoning.

The second antinomy illustrates the dependence of the problem of continuity upon that of infinity. The thesis states : " Every complex substance in the world consists of simple parts, and there exists everywhere nothing but the simple or what is composed of it." The antithesis states : " No complex thing in the world consists of simple parts, and everywhere in it there exists nothing simple." Here, as before, the proofs of both thesis and antithesis are open to criticism, but for the purpose of vindicating physics and the world of sense it is enough to find a fallacy in *one* of the proofs. We will choose for this purpose the proof of the antithesis, which begins as follows :

" Assume that a complex thing (as substance) consists of simple parts. Since all external relation, and therefore all composition out of substances, is only possible in space, the space occupied by a complex thing must consist of as many parts as the thing consists of. Now space does not consist of simple parts, but of spaces."

The rest of his argument need not concern us, for the nerve of the proof lies in the one statement : " Space does not consist of simple parts, but of spaces." This is like Bergson's objection to " the absurd proposition that motion is made up of immobilities." Kant does not tell us why he holds that a space must consist of spaces rather than of simple parts. Geometry regards space as made up of points, which are simple ; and although, as we have seen, this view is not scientifically or logically *necessary*, it remains *prima facie* possible, and its mere possibility is enough to vitiate Kant's argument. For, if his proof of the thesis of the antinomy were valid, and if the antithesis could only be avoided by assuming points, then the antinomy itself would afford a conclusive reason in favour of points. Why, then, did Kant think it impossible that space should be composed of points ?

I think two considerations probably influenced him. In the first place, the essential thing about space is spatial order, and mere points, by themselves, will not account for spatial order. It is obvious that his argument assumes absolute space ; but it is spatial *relations* that are alone important, and they cannot be reduced to points. This ground for his view depends, therefore, upon his ignorance of the logical theory of order and his oscillations between absolute and relative space. But there is also another ground for his opinion, which is more relevant to our present topic. This is the ground derived from infinite divisibility. A space may be halved, and then halved again, and so on *ad infinitum*, and at every stage of the process the parts are still spaces, not points. In order to reach points by such a method, it would be necessary to come to the end of an unending process, which is impossible. But just as an infinite class can be given all at once by its defining concept, though it cannot be reached by successive enumeration, so an infinite set of points can be given all at once as making up a line or area or volume, though they can never be reached by the process of successive division. Thus the infinite divisibility of space gives no ground for deny-ing that space is composed of points. Kant does not give his grounds for this denial, and we can therefore only conjecture what they were. But the above two grounds, which we have seen to be fallacious, seem sufficient to account for his opinion, and we may therefore conclude that the antithesis of the second antinomy is unproved.

The above illustration of Kant's antinomies has only been introduced in order to show the relevance of the problem of infinity to the problem of the reality of objects of sense. In the remainder of the present lecture, I wish to state and explain the problem of infinity, to show how it arose, and to show the irrelevance of all the solutions proposed by philosophers. In the following lecture, I shall try to explain the true solution, which has been discovered by the mathematicians, but nevertheless belongs essentially to philosophy. The solution is definitive, in the sense that it entirely satisfies and convinces all who study it carefully. For over two thousand years the human intellect was baffled by the problem ; its many failures and its ultimate success make this problem peculiarly apt for the illustration of method.

The problem appears to have first arisen in some such way as the following.[1] Pythagoras and his followers, who were interested, like Descartes, in the application of number to geometry, adopted in that science more arithmetical methods than those with which Euclid has made us familiar. They, or their contemporaries the atomists, believed, apparently, that space is composed of indivisible points, while time is composed of indivisible instants.[2] This belief would not, by itself, have raised the difficulties which they encountered, but it was presumably accompanied by another belief, that the number of points in any finite area or of instants in any finite period must be finite. I do not suppose that this latter belief was a conscious one, because probably no other possibility had occurred to them. But the belief nevertheless operated, and

[1] In what concerns the early Greek philosophers, my knowledge is largely derived from Burnet's valuable work, *Early Greek Philosophy* (2nd ed., London, 1908). I have also been greatly assisted by Mr. D. S. Robertson of Trinity College, who has supplied the deficiencies of my knowledge of Greek, and brought important references to my notice.

[2] Cf. Aristotle, *Metaphysics*, M. 6, 1080b, 18 sqq., and 1083b, 8 sqq.

very soon brought them into conflict with facts which they themselves discovered. Before explaining how this occurred, however, it is necessary to say one word in explanation of the phrase "finite number." The *exact* explanation is a matter for our next lecture ; for the present, it must suffice to say that I mean 0 and 1 and 2 and 3 and so one, for ever—in other words, any number that can be obtained by successively adding ones. This includes all the numbers that can be expressed by means of our ordinary numerals, and since such numbers can be made greater and greater, without ever reaching an unsurpassable maximum, it is easy to suppose that there are no other numbers. But this supposition, natural as it is, is mistaken.

Whether the Pythagoreans themselves believed space and time to be composed of indivisible points and instants is a debatable question.[1] It would seem that the distinction between space and matter had

---

[1] There is some reason to think that the Pythagoreans distinguished between discrete and continuous quantity. G. J. Allman, in his *Greek Geometry from Thales to Euclid*, says (p. 23) : "The Pythagoreans made a fourfold division of mathematical science, attributing one of its parts to the how many, τὸ πόσον, and the other to the how much, τὸ πηλίκον ; and they assigned to each of these parts a twofold division. For they said that discrete quantity, or the *how many*, either subsists by itself or must be considered with relation to some other ; but that continued quantity, or the *how much*, is either stable or in motion. Hence they affirmed that arithmetic contemplates that discrete quantity which subsists by itself, but music that which is related to another ; and that geometry considers continued quantity so far as it is immovable ; but astronomy (τὴν σφαιρικήν) contemplates continued quantity so far as it is of a self-motive nature. (Proclus, ed. Friedlein, p. 35. As to the distinction between τὸ πηλίκον, continuous, and τὸ πόσον, discrete quantity, see Iambl., *in Nicomachi Geraseni Arithmeticam introductionem*, ed. Tennulius, p. 148.)" Cf. p. 48.

not yet been clearly made, and that therefore, when an atomistic view is expressed, it is difficult to decide whether particles of matter or points of space are intended. There is an interesting passage [1] in Aristotle's *Physics*,[2] where he says :

" The Pythagoreans all maintained the existence of the void, and said that it enters into the heaven itself from the boundless breath, inasmuch as the heaven breathes in the void also ; and the void differentiates natures, as if it were a sort of separation of consecutives, and as if it were their differentiation ; and that this also is what is first in numbers, for it is the void which differentiates them."

This seems to imply that they regarded matter as consisting of atoms with empty space in between. But if so, they must have thought space could be studied by only paying attention to the atoms, for otherwise it would be hard to account for their arithmetical methods in geometry, or for their statement that " things are numbers."

The difficulty which beset the Pythagoreans in their attempts to apply numbers arose through their discovery of incommensurables, and this, in turn, arose as follows. Pythagoras, as we all learnt in youth, discovered the proposition that the sum of the squares on the sides of a right-angled triangle is equal to the square on the hypotenuse. It is said that he sacrificed an ox when he discovered this theorem ; if so, the ox was the first martyr to science. But the theorem, though it has remained his chief claim to immortality, was soon found to have a consequence fatal to his

[1] Referred to by Burnet, op. cit., p. 120.
[2] iv., 6. 213*b*, 22 ; H. Ritter and L. Preller, *Historia Philosophiæ Græcæ*, 8th ed., Gotha, 1898, p. 75 (this work will be referred to in future as " R. P.").

whole philosophy.   Consider the case of a right-angled triangle whose two sides are equal, such a triangle as is formed by two sides of a square and a diagonal. Here, in virtue of the theorem, the square on the diagonal is double of the square on either of the sides. But Pythagoras or his early followers easily proved that the square of one whole number cannot be double of the square of another.[1] Thus the length of the side and the length of the diagonal are incommensurable ; that is to say, however small a unit of length you take, if it is contained an exact number of times in the side, it is not contained any exact number of times in the diagonal, and *vice versa*.

Now this fact might have been assimilated by some philosophies without any great difficulty, but to the philosophy of Pythagoras it was absolutely fatal. Pythagoras held that number is the constitutive essence of all things, yet no two numbers could express the ratio of the side of a square to the diagonal.   It would seem probable that we may expand his difficulty, without departing from his thought, by assuming that he regarded the length of a line as determined by the number of atoms contained in it—a line two inches long would contain twice as many atoms as a line one inch long, and so on.   But if this were the truth, then there must be a definite numerical ratio between

---

[1] The Pythagorean proof is roughly as follows.   If possible, let the ratio of the diagonal to the side of a square be m/n, where m and n are whole numbers having no common factor. Then we must have $m^2 = 2n^2$. Now the square of an odd number is odd, but m^2, being equal to $2n^2$, is even.   Hence m must be even.   But the square of an even number divides by 4, therefore n^2, which is half of m^2, must be even.   Therefore n must be even.   But, since m is even, and m and n have no common factor, n must be odd.   Thus n must be both odd and even, which is impossible ; and therefore the diagonal and the side cannot have a rational ratio.

any two finite lengths, because it was supposed that the number of atoms in each, however large, must be finite. Here there was an insoluble contradiction. The Pythagoreans, it is said, resolved to keep the existence of incommensurables a profound secret, revealed only to a few of the supreme heads of the sect ; and one of their number, Hippasos of Meta-pontion, is even said to have been shipwrecked at sea for impiously disclosing the terrible discovery to their enemies. It must be remembered that Pytha-goras was the founder of a new religion as well as the teacher of a new science : if the science came to be doubted, the disciples might fall into sin, and perhaps even eat beans, which according to Pythagoras is as bad as eating parents' bones.

The problem first raised by the discovery of incom-mensurables proved, as time went on, to be one of the most severe and at the same time most far-reaching problems that have confronted the human intellect in its endeavour to understand the world. It showed at once that numerical measurement of lengths, if it was to be made accurate, must require an arithmetic more advanced and more difficult than any that the ancients possessed. They therefore set to work to reconstruct geometry on a basis which did not assume the universal possibility of numerical measurement— a reconstruction which, as may be seen in Euclid, they effected with extraordinary skill and with great logical acumen. The moderns, under the influence of Cartesian geometry, have reasserted the universal possibility of numerical measurement, extending arith-metic, partly for that purpose, so as to include what are called " irrational " numbers, which give the ratios of incommensurable lengths. But although irrational numbers have long been used without a qualm, it is only in quite recent years that logically satisfactory definitions of them have been given. With these definitions, the first and most obvious form of the difficulty which confronted the Pythagoreans has been solved ; but other forms of the difficulty remain to be considered, and it is these that introduce us to the problem of infinity in its pure form.

We saw that, accepting the view that a length is composed of points, the existence of incommensurables proves that every finite length must contain an infinite number of points. In other words, if we were to take away points one by one, we should never have taken away all the points, however long we continued the process. The number of points therefore, cannot be *counted*, for counting is a process which enumerates things one by one. The property of being unable to be counted is characteristic of infinite collections, and is a source of many of their paradoxical qualities. So paradoxical are these qualities that until our own day they were thought to constitute logical contradictions. A long line of philosophers, from Zeno [1] to M. Bergson, have based much of their metaphysics upon the supposed impossibility of infinite collections. Broadly speaking, the difficulties were stated by Zeno, and nothing material was added until we reach Bolzano's *Paradoxien des Unendlichlen*, a little work written in 1847–8, and published posthumously in 1851. Intervening attempts to deal with the problem are futile and negligible. The definitive solution of the difficulties is due, not to Bolzano, but to Georg Cantor, whose work on this subject first appeared in 1882.

[1] In regard to Zeno and the Pythagoreans, I have derived much valuable information and criticism from Mr. P. E. B Jourdain.

In order to understand Zeno, and to realize how little modern orthodox metaphysics has added to the achievements of the Greeks, we must consider for a moment his master Parmenides, in whose interest the paradoxes were invented.[1] Parmenídes expounded his views in a poem divided into two parts, called " the way of truth " and " the way of opinion "— like Mr. Bradley's " Appearance " and " Reality," except that Parmenides tells us first about reality and then about appearance. " The way of opinion," in his philosophy, is, broadly speaking, Pythagoreanism ; it begins with a warning : " Here I shall close my trustworthy speech and thought about the truth. Henceforward learn the opinions of mortals, giving ear to the deceptive ordering of my words." What has gone before has been revealed by a goddess, who tells him what really *is*. Reality, she says, is uncreated, indestructible, unchanging, indivisible ; it is " immovable in the bonds of mighty chains, without beginning and without end ; since coming into being and passing away have been driven afar, and true belief has cast them away." The fundamental principle of his inquiry is stated in a sentence which would not be out of place in Hegel : [2] " Thou canst not know what is not—that is impossible—nor utter it ; for it is the same thing that can be thought and that can be." And again : " It needs must be that what can be thought and spoken of is ; for it is possible for it to be, and it is not possible for what is nothing to be." The impossibility of change follows from this principle ;

---

[1] So Plato makes Zeno say in the *Parmenides*, apropos of his philosophy as a whole ; and all internal and external evidence supports this view.

[2] " With Parmenides," Hegel says, " philosophizing proper began." *Werke* (edition of 1840), vol. xiii. p. 274.

for what is past can be spoken of, and therefore, by the principle, still is.

The great conception of a reality behind the passing illusions of sense, a reality one, indivisible, and unchanging, was thus introduced into Western philosophy by Parmenides, not, it would seem, for mystical or religious reasons, but on the basis of a logical argument as to the impossibility of not-being. All the great metaphysical systems—notably those of Plato, Spinoza, and Hegel—are the outcome of this fundamental idea. It is difficult to disentangle the truth and the error in this view. The contention that time is unreal and that the world of sense is illusory must, I think, be regarded as based upon fallacious reasoning. Nevertheless, there is some sense—easier to feel than to state—in which time is an unimportant and superficial characteristic of reality. Past and future must be acknowledged to be as real as the present, and a certain emancipation from slavery to time is essential to philosophic thought. The importance of time is rather practical than theoretical, rather in relation to our desires than in relation to truth. A truer image of the world, I think, is obtained by picturing things as entering into the stream of time from an eternal world outside, than from a view which regards time as the devouring tyrant of all that is. Both in thought and in feeling, to realize the unimportance of time is the gate of wisdom. But unimportance is not unreality ; and therefore what we shall have to say about Zeno's arguments in support of Parmenides must be mainly critical.

The relation of Zeno to Parmenides is explained by Plato [1] in the dialogue in which Socrates, as a young man, learns logical acumen and philosophic dis-

[1] *Parmenides*, 128 A–D.

interestedness from their dialectic. I quote from Jowett's translation :

" I see, Parmenides, said Socrates, that Zeno is your second self in his writings too ; he puts what you say in another way, and would fain deceive us into believing that he is telling us what is new. For you, in your poems, say All is one, and of this you adduce excellent proofs ; and he on the other hand says There is no Many ; and on behalf of this he offers overwhelming evidence. To deceive the world, as you have done, by saying the same thing in different ways, one of you affirming the one, and the other denying the many, is a strain of art beyond the reach of most of us.

" Yes, Socrates, said Zeno. But although you are as keen as a Spartan hound in pursuing the track, you do not quite apprehend the true motive of the composition, which is not really such an ambitious work as you imagine ; for what you speak of was an accident ; I had no serious intention of deceiving the world. The truth is that these writings of mine were meant to protect the arguments of Parmenides against those who scoff at him and show the many ridiculous and contradictory results which they suppose to follow from the affirmation of the one. My answer is an address to the partisans of the many, whose attack I return with interest by retorting upon them that their hypothesis of the being of the many if carried out appears in a still more ridiculous light than the hypothesis of the being of the one."

Zeno's four arguments against motion were intended to exhibit the contradictions that result from supposing that there is such a thing as change, and thus to support the Parmenidean doctrine that reality is unchanging.[1]

[1] This interpretation is combated by Milhaud, *Les philo-*

Unfortunately, we only know his arguments through Aristotle,[1] who stated them in order to refute them. Those philosophers in the present day who have had their doctrines stated by opponents will realize that a just or adequate presentation of Zeno's position is hardly to be expected from Aristotle ; but by some care in interpretation it seems possible to reconstruct the so-called " sophisms " which have been " refuted " by every tyro from that day to this.

Zeno's arguments would seem to be " ad hominem " ; that is to say, they seem to assume premisses granted by his opponents, and to show that, granting these premisses, it is possible to deduce consequences which his opponents must deny. In order to decide whether they are valid arguments or " sophisms," it is necessary to guess at the tacit premisses, and to decide who was the " homo " at whom they were aimed. Some maintain that they were aimed at the Pythagoreans,[2] while others have held that they were intended to refute the atomists.[3] M. Evellin, on the contrary, holds that they constitute a refutation of infinite divisibility,[4] while M. G. Noël, in the interests of Hegel, maintains that the first two arguments refute

sophes-géomètres de la Grèce, p. 140 n., but his reasons do not seem to me convincing. All the interpretations in what follows are open to question, but all have the support of reputable authorities.

[1] Physics, vi. 9. 2396 (R.P. 136–139).

[2] Cf. Gaston Milhaud, Les philosophes-géomètres de la Grèce, p. 140 n. ; Paul Tannery, Pour l'histoire de la science hellène, p. 249 ; Burnet, op. cit., p. 362.

[3] Cf. R. K. Gaye, " On Aristotle, Physics, Z ix." Journal of Philology, vol. xxxi. esp. p. 111. Also Moritz Cantor, Vorlesungen über Geschichte der Mathematik, 1st ed., vol. i., 1880, p. 168, who, however, subsequently adopted Paul Tannery's opinion, Vorlesungen, 3rd ed. (vol. i. p. 200).

[4] " Le mouvement et les partisans des indivisibles," Revue de Métaphysique et de Morale, vol. i. pp. 382–395.

infinite divisibility, while the next two refute indivisibles.[1] Amid such a bewildering variety of interpretations, we can at least not complain of any restrictions on our liberty of choice.

The historical questions raised by the above-mentioned discussions are no doubt largely insoluble, owing to the very scanty material from which our evidence is derived. The points which seem fairly clear are the following : (1) That, in spite of MM. Milhaud and Paul Tannery, Zeno is anxious to prove that motion is really impossible, and that he desires to prove this because he follows Parmenides in denying plurality ; [2] (2) that the third and fourth arguments proceed on the hypothesis of indivisibles, a hypothesis which, whether adopted by the Pythagoreans or not, was certainly much advocated, as may be seen from the treatise *On Indivisible Lines* attributed to Aristotle. As regards the first two arguments, they would seem to be valid on the hypothesis of indivisibles, and also, without this hypothesis, to be such as would be valid if the traditional contradictions in infinite numbers were insoluble, which they are not.

We may conclude, therefore, that Zeno's polemic is directed against the view that space and time consist of points and instants ; and that as against the view that a finite stretch of space of time consists of a finite number of points and instants, his arguments are not sophisms, but perfectly valid.

The conclusion which Zeno wishes us to draw is that plurality is a delusion, and spaces and times are really indivisible. The other conclusion which is possible,

[1] " Le mouvement et les arguments de Zénon d'Élée," *Revue de Métaphysique et de Morale*, vol. i. pp. 107–125.

[2] Cf. N. Brochard, " Les prétendus sophismes de Zénon d'Élée," *Revue de Métaphysique et de Morale*, vol. i. pp. 209–215.

namely that the number of points and instants is infinite, was not tenable so long as the infinite was infected with contradictions. In a fragment which is not one of the four famous arguments against motion, Zeno says :

" If things are a many, they must be just as many as they are, and neither more nor less. Now, if they are as many as they are, they will be finite in number.

" If things are a many, they will be infinite in number ; for there will always be other things between them, and others again between these. And so things are infinite in number." [1]

This argument attempts to prove that, if there are many things, the number of them must be both finite and infinite, which is impossible ; hence we are to conclude that there is only one thing. But the weak point in the argument is the phrase : " If they are just as many as they are, they will be finite in number." This phrase is not very clear, but it is plain that it assumes the impossibility of definite infinite numbers. Without this assumption, which is now known to be false, the arguments of Zeno, though they suffice (on certain very reasonable assumptions) to dispel the hypothesis of finite indivisibles, do not suffice to prove that motion and change and plurality are impossible. They are not, however, on any view, mere foolish quibbles : they are serious arguments, raising difficulties which it has taken two thousand years to answer, and which even now are fatal to the teachings of most philosophers.

The first of Zeno's arguments is the argument of

---

[1] Simplicius, *Phys.*, 140, 28 D (R.P. 133) ; Burnet, op. cit., pp. 364–365.

the race-course, which is paraphrased by Burnet as follows : [1]

" You cannot get to the end of a race-course. You cannot traverse an infinite number of points in a finite time. You must traverse the half of any given distance before you traverse the whole, and the half of that again before you can traverse it. This goes on *ad infinitum*, so that there are an infinite number of points in any given space, and you cannot touch an infinite number one by one in a finite time." [2]

Zeno appeals here, in the first place, to the fact that any distance, however small, can be halved. From this it follows, of course, that there must be an infinite number of points in a line. But Aristotle represents

[1] Op. cit., p. 367.
[2] Aristotle's words are : " The first is the one on the non-existence of motion on the ground that what is moved must always attain the middle point sooner than the end-point, on which we gave our opinion in the earlier part of our discourse." *Phys.*, vi. 9. 939B (R.P. 136). Aristotle seems to refer to *Phys.*, vi. 2. 223AB [R.P. 136A] : " All space is continuous, for time and space are divided into the same and equal divisions. . . . Wherefore also Zeno's argument is fallacious, that it is impossible to go through an infinite collection or to touch an infinite collection one by one in a finite time. For there are two senses in which the term ' infinite ' is applied both to length and to time, and in fact to all continuous things, either in regard to divisibility, or in regard to the ends. Now it is not possible to touch things infinite in regard to number in a finite time, but it is possible to touch things infinite in regard to divisibility : for time itself also is infinite in this sense. So that in fact we go through an infinite [space], in an infinite [time] and not in a finite [time], and we touch infinite things with infinite things, not with finite things." Philoponus, a sixth-century commentator (R.P. 136A, *Exc. Paris Philop. in Arist. Phys.*, 803, 2. Vit.), gives the following illustration : " For if a thing were moved the space of a cubit in one hour, since in every space there are an infinite number of points, the thing moved must needs touch all the points of the space : it will then go through an infinite collection in a finite time, which is impossible."

him as arguing, you cannot touch an infinite number of points *one by one* in a finite time. The words " one by one " are important. (1) If *all* the points touched are concerned, then, though you pass through them continuously, you do not touch them " one by one." That is to say, after touching one, there is not another which you touch next : no two points are next each other, but between any two there are always an infinite number of others, which cannot be enumerated one by one. (2) If, on the other hand, only the successive middle points are concerned, obtained by always halving what remains of the course, then the points are reached one by one, and, though they are infinite in number, they are in fact all reached in a finite time. His argument to the contrary may be supposed to appeal to the view that a finite time must consist of a finite number of instants, in which case what he says would be perfectly true on the assumption that the possibility of continued dichotomy is undeniable. If, on the other hand, we suppose the argument directed against the partisans of infinite divisibility, we must suppose it to proceed as follows : [1] " The points given by successive halving of the distances still to be traversed are infinite in number, and are reached in succession, each being reached a finite time later than its predecessor ; but the sum of an infinite number of finite times must be infinite, and therefore the process will never be completed." It is very possible that this is historically the right inter-pretation, but in this form the argument is invalid. If half the course takes half a minute, and the next quarter takes a quarter of a minute, and so on, the whole course will take a minute. The apparent

[1] Cf. Mr. C. D. Broad, " Note on Achilles and the Tortoise,' *Mind*, N.S., vol. xxii. pp. 318–9.

force of the argument, on this interpretation, lies solely in the mistaken supposition that there cannot be anything between the whole of an infinite series, which can be seen to be false by observing that 1 is beyond the whole of the infinite series, $\frac{1}{2}, \frac{3}{4}, \frac{7}{8}, \frac{15}{16}, \ldots$

The second of Zeno's arguments is the one concerning Achilles and the tortoise, which has achieved more notoriety than the others. It is paraphrased by Burnet as follows : [1]

" Achilles will never overtake the tortoise. He must first reach the place from which the tortoise started. By that time the tortoise will have got some way ahead. Achilles must then make up that, and again the tortoise will be ahead. He is always coming nearer, but he never makes up to it." [2]

This argument is essentially the same as the previous one. It shows that, if Achilles ever overtakes the tortoise, it must be after an infinite number of instants have elapsed since he started. This is in fact true ; but the view that an infinite number of instants make up an infinitely long time is not true, and therefore the conclusion that Achilles will never overtake the tortoise does not follow.

The third argument,[3] that of the arrow, is very interesting. The text has been questioned. Burnet accepts the alterations of Zeller, and paraphrases thus :

[1] Op. cit.

[2] Aristotle's words are: " The second is the so-called Achilles. It consists in this, that the slower will never be overtaken in its course by the quickest, for the pursuer must always come first to the point from which the pursued has just departed, so that the slower must necessarily be always still more or less in advance." *Phys.*, vi. 9. 239B (R.P. 137).

[3] *Phys.*, vi. 9. 239B (R.P. 138).

" The arrow in flight is at rest.   For, if everything is at rest when it occupies a space equal to
itself, and what is in flight at any given moment
always occupies a space equal to itself, it cannot
move."

But according to Prantl, the literal translation
of the unemended text of Aristotle's statement of the
argument is as follows : " If everything, when it is
behaving in a uniform manner, is continually either
moving or at rest, but what is moving is always in
the *now*, then the moving arrow is motionless."   This
form of the argument brings out its force more clearly
than Burnet's paraphrase.

Here, if not in the first two arguments, the view that
a finite part of time consists of a finite series of successive instants seems to be assumed ; at any rate
the plausibility of the argument seems to depend upon
supposing that there are consecutive instants.
Throughout an instant, it is said, a moving body is
where it is : it cannot move during the instant, for
that would require that the instant should have parts.
Thus, suppose we consider a period consisting of a
thousand instants, and suppose the arrow is in flight
throughout this period.   At each of the thousand
instants, the arrow is where it is, though at the next
instant it is somewhere else.   It is never moving,
but in some miraculous way the change of position
has to occur *between* the instants, that is to say, not
at any time whatever.   This is what M. Bergson calls
the cinematographic representation of reality.   The
more the difficulty is meditated, the more real it
becomes.   The solution lies in the theory of continuous
series : we find it hard to avoid supposing that, when
the arrow is in flight, there is a *next* position occupied
at the *next* moment ; but in fact there is no next

position and no next moment, and when once this is imaginatively realized, the difficulty is seen to disappear.

The fourth and last of Zeno's arguments is [1] the argument of the stadium.

The argument as stated by Burnet is as follows :

First Position.	Second Position.
A	A . . . .
B	B . . . .
C	C . . . .

" Half the time may be equal to double the time. Let us suppose three rows of bodies, one of which (A) is at rest while the other two (B, C) are moving with equal velocity in opposite directions. By the time they are all in the same part of the course, B will have passed twice as many of the bodies in C as in A. Therefore the time which it takes to pass C is twice as long as the time it takes to pass A. But the time which B and C take to reach the position of A is the same. Therefore double the time is equal to the half."

Gaye [2] devoted an interesting article to the interpretation of this argument. His translation of Aristotle's statement is as follows :

" The fourth argument is that concerning the two rows of bodies, each row being composed of an equal number of bodies of equal size, passing each other on a race-course as they proceed with equal velocity in opposite directions, the one row originally occupying the space between the goal and the middle point of the course, and the other that between the middle

---

[1] *Phys.*, vi. 9. 239B (R.P. 139).
[2] Loc. cit.

point and the starting-post. This, he thinks, involves the conclusion that half a given time is equal to double the time. The fallacy of the reasoning lies in the assumption that a body occupies an equal time in passing with equal velocity a body that is in motion and a body of equal size that is at rest, an assumption which is false. For instance (so runs the argument), let A A . . . be the stationary bodies of equal size, B B . . . the bodies, equal in number and in size to A A . . ., originally occupying the half of the course from the starting-post to the middle of the A's, and C C . . . those originally occupying the other half from the goal to the middle of the A's, equal in number, size, and velocity, to B B . . . Then three consequences follow. First, as the B's and C's pass one another, the first B reaches the last C at the same moment at which the first C reaches the last B. Secondly, at this moment the first C has passed all the A's, whereas the first B has passed only half the A's and has consequently occupied only half the time occupied by the first C, since each of the two occupies an equal time in passing each A. Thirdly, at the same moment all the B's have passed all the C's : for the first C and the first B will simultaneously reach the opposite ends of the course, since (so says Zeno) the time occupied by the first C in passing each of the B's is equal to that occupied by it in passing each of the A's, because an equal time is occupied by both the first B and the first C in passing all the A's. This is the argument : but it presupposes the aforesaid fallacious assumption."

This argument is not quite easy to follow, and it is only valid as against the assumption that a finite time consists of a finite number of instants. We may re-state it in different language. Let us

suppose three drill-sergeants, A, A', and A'', standing in
a row, while the two files of soldiers march past them in

First Position.				Second Position.		
B	B'	B''		B	B'	B''
·	·	·		·	·	·
A	A'	A''		A	A'	A''
·	·	·		·	·	·
C	C'	C''		C	C'	C''
·	·	·		·	·	·

opposite directions. At the first moment which we
consider, the three men B, B', B'' in one row, and the
three men C, C', C'' in the other row, are respectively
opposite to A, A', and A''. At the very next moment,
each row has moved on, and now B and C'' are opposite
A'. Thus B and C'' are opposite each other. When,
then, did B pass C'? It must have been somewhere
between the two moments which we supposed consecutive, and therefore the two moments cannot really
have been consecutive. It follows that there must
be other moments between any two given moments,
and therefore that there must be an infinite number of
moments in any given interval of time.

The above difficulty, that B must have passed C'
at some time between two consecutive moments, is a
genuine one, but is not precisely the difficulty raised by
Zeno. What Zeno professes to prove is that " half of
a given time is equal to double that time." The most
intelligible explanation of the argument known to me
is that of Gaye.[1] Since, however, his explanation is
not easy to set forth shortly, I will re-state what
seems to me to be the logical essence of Zeno's contention. If we suppose that time consists of a series of

[1] Loc. cit., p. 105.

consecutive instants, and that motion consists in passing through a series of consecutive points, then the fastest possible motion is one which, at each instant, is at a point consecutive to that at which it was at the previous instant. Any slower motion must be one which has intervals of rest interspersed, and any faster motion must wholly omit some points. All this is evident from the fact that we cannot have more than one event for each instant. But now, in the case of our A's and B's and C's, B is opposite a fresh A every instant, and therefore the number of A's passed gives the number of instants since the beginning of the motion. But during the motion B has passed twice as many C's, and yet cannot have passed more than one each instant. Hence the number of instants since the motion began is twice the number of A's passed, though we previously found it was equal to this number. From this result, Zeno's conclusion follows.

Zeno's arguments, in some form, have afforded grounds for almost all the theories of space and time and infinity which have been constructed from his day to our own. We have seen that all his arguments are valid (with certain reasonable hypotheses) on the assumption that finite spaces and times consist of a finite number of points and instants, and that the third and fourth almost certainly in fact proceeded on this assumption, while the first and second, which were perhaps intended to refute the opposite assumption, were in that case fallacious. We may therefore escape from his paradoxes either by maintaining that, though space and time do consist of points and instants, the number of them in any finite interval is infinite ; or by denying that space and time consist of points and instants at all ; or lastly, by denying the reality of space and time altogether. It would seem that Zeno himself, as a supporter of Parmenides, drew the last of these three possible deductions, at any rate in regard to time. In this a very large number of philosophers have followed him. Many others, like M. Bergson, have preferred to deny that space and time consist of points and instants. Either of these solutions will meet the difficulties in the form in which Zeno raised them. But, as we saw, the difficulties can also be met if infinite numbers are admissible. And on grounds which are independent of space and time, infinite numbers, and series in which no two terms are consecutive, must in any case be admitted. Consider, for example, all the fractions less than 1, arranged in order of magnitude. Between any two of them, there are others, for example, the arithmetical mean of the two. Thus no two fractions are consecutive, and the total number of them is infinite. It will be found that much of what Zeno says as regards the series of points on a line can be equally well applied to the series of fractions. And we cannot deny that there are fractions, so that two of the above ways of escape are closed to us. It follows that, if we are to solve the whole class of difficulties derivable from Zeno's by analogy, we must discover some tenable theory of infinite numbers. What, then, are the difficulties which, until the last thirty years, led philosophers to the belief that infinite numbers are impossible ?

The difficulties of infinity are of two kinds, of which the first may be called sham, while the others involve, for their solution, a certain amount of new and not altogether easy thinking. The sham difficulties are those suggested by the etymology, and those suggested by confusion of the mathematical infinite with what philosophers impertinently call the " true " infinite.

Etymologically, "infinite" should mean "having no end." But in fact some infinite series have ends, some have not; while some collections are infinite without being serial, and can therefore not properly be regarded as either endless or having ends. The series of instants from any earlier one to any later one (both included) is infinite, but has two ends; the series of instants from the beginning of time to the present moment has one end, but is infinite. Kant, in his first antinomy, seems to hold that it is harder for the past to be infinite than for the future to be so, on the ground that the past is now completed, and that nothing infinite can be completed. It is very difficult to see how he can have imagined that there was any sense in this remark; but it seems most probable that he was thinking of the infinite as the "unended." It is odd that he did not see that the future too has one end at the present, and is precisely on a level with the past. His regarding the two as different in this respect illustrates just that kind of slavery to time which, as we agreed in speaking of Parmenides, the true philosopher must learn to leave behind him.

The confusions introduced into the notions of philosophers by the so-called "true" infinite are curious. They see that this notion is not the same as the mathematical infinite, but they choose to believe that it is the notion which the mathematicians are vainly trying to reach. They therefore inform the mathematicians, kindly but firmly, that they are mistaken in adhering to the "false" infinite, since plainly the "true" infinite is something quite different. The reply to this is that what they call the "true" infinite is a notion totally irrelevant to the problem of the mathematical infinite, to which it has only a fanciful and verbal analogy. So remote is it that I do not propose to confuse the issue by even mentioning what the " true " infinite is. It is the " false " infinite that concerns us, and we have to show that the epithet " false " is undeserved.

There are, however, certain genuine difficulties in understanding the infinite, certain habits of mind derived from the consideration of finite numbers, and easily extended to infinite numbers under the mistaken notion that they represent logical necessities. For example, every number that we are accustomed to, except 0, has another number immediately before it, from which it results by adding 1 ; but the first infinite number does not have this property. The numbers before it form an infinite series, containing all the ordinary finite numbers, having no maximum, no last finite number, after which one little step would plunge us into the infinite. If it is assumed that the first infinite number is reached by a succession of small steps, it is easy to show that it is self-contradictory. The first infinite number is, in fact, beyond the whole unending series of finite numbers. " But," it will be said, " there cannot be anything beyond the whole of an unending series." This, we may point out, is the very principle upon which Zeno relies in the arguments of the race-course and the Achilles. Take the race-course : there is the moment when the runner still has half his distance to run, then the moment when he still has a quarter, then when he still has an eighth, and so on in a strictly unending series. Beyond the whole of this series is the moment when he reaches the goal. Thus there certainly can be something beyond the whole of an unending series. But it remains to show that this fact is only what might have been expected.

The difficulty, like most of the vaguer difficulties besetting the mathematical infinite, is derived, I think, from the more or less unconscious operation of the idea of *counting*. If you set to work to count the terms in an infinite collection, you will never have completed your task. Thus, in the case of the runner, if half, three-quarters, seven-eighths, and so on of the course were marked, and the runner was not allowed to pass any of the marks until the umpire said " Now," then Zeno's conclusion would be true in practice, and he would never reach the goal.

But it is not essential to the existence of a collection, or even to knowledge and reasoning concerning it, that we should be able to pass its terms in review one by one. This may be seen in the case of finite collections ; we can speak of " mankind " or " the human race," though many of the individuals in this collection are not personally known to us. We can do this because we know of various characteristics which every individual has if he belongs to the collection, and not if he does not. And exactly the same happens in the case of infinite collections : they may be known by their characteristics although their terms cannot be enumerated. In this sense, an unending series may nevertheless form a whole, and there may be new terms beyond the whole of it.

Some purely arithmetical peculiarities of infinite numbers have also caused perplexity. For instance, an infinite number is not increased by adding one to it, or by doubling it. Such peculiarities have seemed to many to contradict logic, but in fact they only contradict confirmed mental habits. The whole difficulty of the subject lies in the necessity of thinking in an unfamiliar way, and in realizing that many properties which we have thought inherent in number are in fact peculiar to finite numbers. If this is remembered, the positive theory of infinity, which will occupy the next lecture, will not be found so difficult as it is to those who cling obstinately to the prejudices instilled by the arithmetic which is learnt in childhood.

LECTURE VII

THE POSITIVE THEORY OF INFINITY

THE positive theory of infinity, and the general theory of number to which it has given rise, are among the triumphs of scientific method in philosophy, and are therefore specially suitable for illustrating the logical-analytic character of that method. The work in this subject has been done by mathematicians, and its results can be expressed in mathematical symbolism. Why, then, it may be said, should the subject be regarded as philosophy rather than as mathematics? This raises a difficult question, partly concerned with the use of words, but partly also of real importance in understanding the function of philosophy. Every subject-matter, it would seem, can give rise to philosophical investigations as well as to the appropriate science, the difference between the two treatments being in the direction of movement and in the kind of truths which it is sought to establish. In the special sciences, when they have become fully developed, the movement is forward and synthetic, from the simpler to the more complex. But in philosophy we follow the inverse direction : from the complex and relatively concrete we proceed towards the simple and abstract by means of analysis, seeking, in the process, to eliminate the particularity of the original subject-matter, and to confine our attention entirely to the logical *form* of the facts concerned.

Between philosophy and pure mathematics there is a certain affinity, in the fact that both are general and *a priori*. Neither of them asserts propositions which, like those of history and geography, depend upon the actual concrete facts being just what they are. We may illustrate this characteristic by means of Leibniz's conception of many *possible* worlds, of which one only is *actual*. In all the many possible worlds, philosophy and mathematics will be the same ; the differences will only be in respect of those particular facts which are chronicled by the descriptive sciences. Any quality, therefore, by which our actual world is distinguished from other abstractly possible worlds, must be ignored by mathematics and philosophy alike. Mathematics and philosophy differ, however, in their manner of treating the general properties in which all possible worlds agree ; for while mathematics, starting from comparatively simple propositions, seeks to build up more and more complex results by deductive synthesis, philosophy, starting from data which are common knowledge, seeks to purify and generalize them into the simplest statements of abstract form that can be obtained from them by logical analysis.

The difference between philosophy and mathematics may be illustrated by our present problem, namely the nature of number. Both start from certain facts about numbers which are evident to inspection. But mathematics uses these facts to deduce more and more complicated theorems, while philosophy seeks, by analysis, to go behind these facts to others, simpler, more fundamental, and inherently more fitted to form the premisses of the science of arithmetic. The question, " What is a number ? " is the pre-eminent philosophic question in this subject, but it is one which the mathematician as such need not ask, provided he knows enough of the properties of numbers to enable him to deduce his theorems. We, since our object is philosophical, must grapple with the philosopher's question. The answer to the question, " What is a number ? " which we shall reach in this lecture, will be found to give also, by implication, the answer to the difficulties of infinity which we considered in the previous lecture.

The question " What is a number ? " is one which, until quite recent times, was never considered in the kind of way that is capable of yielding a precise answer. Philosophers were content with some vague dictum such as " Number is unity in plurality." A typical definition of the kind that contented philosophers is the following from Sigwart's *Logic* (§ 66, section 3) : " Every number is not merely a *plurality*, but a plurality thought *as held together and closed, and to that extent as a unity*." Now there is in such definitions a very elementary blunder, of the same kind that would be committed if we said " yellow is a flower " because some flowers are yellow. Take, for example, the number 3. A single collection of three things might conceivably be described as " a plurality thought as held together and closed, and to that extent as a unity " ; but a collection of three things is not the number 3. The number 3 is something which all collections of three things have in common, but is not itself a collection of three things. The definition, therefore, apart from any other defects, has failed to reach the necessary degree of abstraction : the number 3 is something more abstract than any collection of three things.

Such vague philosophic definitions, however, remained inoperative because of their very vagueness. What most men who thought about numbers really had in mind was that numbers are the result of *counting*. " On the consciousness of the law of counting," says Sigwart at the beginning of his discussion of number, " rests the possibility of spontaneously prolonging the series of numbers *ad infinitum*." It is this view of number as generated by counting which has been the chief psychological obstacle to the understanding of infinite numbers. Counting, because it is familiar, is erroneously supposed to be simple, whereas it is in fact a highly complex process, which has no meaning unless the numbers reached in counting have some significance independent of the process by which they are reached. And infinite numbers cannot be reached at all in this way. The mistake is of the same kind as if cows were defined as what can be bought from a cattle-merchant. To a person who knew several cattle-merchants, but had never seen a cow, this might seem an admirable definition. But if in his travels he came across a herd of wild cows, he would have to declare that they were not cows at all, because no cattle-merchant could sell them. So infinite numbers were declared not to be numbers at all, because they could not be reached by counting.

It will be worth while to consider for a moment what counting actually is. We count a set of objects when we let our attention pass from one to another, until we have attended once to each, saying the names of the numbers in order with each successive act of attention. The last number named in this process is the number of the objects, and therefore counting is a method of finding out what the number of the objects is. But this operation is really a very complicated one, and those who imagine that it is the logical source of number show themselves remarkably incapable of analysis. In the first place, when we say " one, two, three . . . " as we count, we cannot be said to be discovering the number of the objects counted unless we attach some meaning to the words one, two, three. . . . A child may learn to know these words in order, and to repeat them correctly like the letters of the alphabet, without attaching any meaning to them. Such a child may count correctly from the point of view of a grown-up listener, without having any idea of numbers at all. The operation of counting, in fact, can only be intelligently performed by a person who already has some idea what the numbers are ; and from this it follows that counting does not give the logical basis of number.

Again, how do we know that the last number reached in the process of counting is the number of the objects counted ? This is just one of those facts that are too familiar for their significance to be realized ; but those who wish to be logicians must acquire the habit of dwelling upon such facts. There are two propositions involved in this fact : first, that the number of numbers from 1 up to any given number is that given number—for instance, the number of numbers from 1 to 100 is a hundred ; secondly, that if a set of numbers can be used as names of a set of objects, each number occurring only once, then the number of numbers used as names is the same as the number of objects. The first of these propositions is capable of an easy arithmetical proof so long as finite numbers are concerned ; but with infinite numbers, after the first, it ceases to be true. The second proposition remains true, and is in fact, as we shall see, an immediate consequence of the definition of number. But owing to the falsehood of the first proposition where infinite numbers are concerned, counting, even if it were practically possible, would not be a valid method of discovering the number of terms in an infinite collection, and would in fact give different results according to the manner in which it was carried out.

There are two respects in which the infinite numbers that are known differ from finite numbers : first, infinite numbers have, while finite numbers have not, a property which I shall call *reflexiveness* ; secondly, finite numbers have, while infinite numbers have not, a property which I shall call *inductiveness*. Let us consider these two properties successively.

(1) *Reflexiveness.*—A number is said to be *reflexive* when it is not increased by adding 1 to it. It follows at once that any finite number can be added to a reflexive number without increasing it. This property of infinite numbers was always thought, until recently, to be self-contradictory ; but through the work of Georg Cantor it has come to be recognized that, though at first astonishing, it is no more self-contradictory than the fact that people at the antipodes do not tumble off. In virtue of this property, given any infinite collection of objects, any finite number of objects can be added or taken away without increasing or diminishing the number of the collection. Even an infinite number of objects may, under certain conditions, be added or taken away without altering the number. This may be made clearer by the help of some examples.

Imagine all the natural numbers 0, 1, 2, 3 . . . to be written down in a row, and immediately beneath them

$$0, 1, 2, 3, \ldots n \ldots$$
$$1, 2, 3, 4, \ldots n + 1 \ldots$$

write down the numbers 1, 2, 3, 4, . . ., so that 1 is under 0, 2 is under 1, and so on.   Then every number in the top row has a number directly under it in the bottom row, and no number occurs twice in either row.   It follows that the number of numbers in the two rows must be the same.   But all the numbers that occur in the bottom row also occur in the top row, and one more, namely 0 ; thus the number of terms in the top row is obtained by adding one to the number of the bottom row.   So long, therefore, as it was supposed that a number must be increased by adding 1 to it, this state of things constituted a contradiction, and led to the denial that there are infinite numbers.

The following example is even more surprising. Write the natural numbers 1, 2, 3, 4 . . . in the top row, and the even numbers 2, 4, 6, 8 . . . in the bottom row, so that under each number in the top row stands its double in the bottom row.   Then, as before, the number of numbers in the two rows is the same, yet the second row results from taking away all the odd numbers—an infinite collection—from the top row.   This example is given by Leibniz to prove that there can be no infinite numbers.   He believed in infinite collections, but, since he thought that a number must always be increased when it is added to and diminished when it is subtracted from, he maintained that infinite collections do not have numbers. " The number of all numbers," he says, " implies a contradiction, which I show thus : To any number there is a corresponding number equal to its double. Therefore the number of all numbers is not greater than the number of even numbers, i.e. the whole is not greater than its part." [1]   In dealing with this

---

[1] *Phil. Werke*, Gerhardt's edition, vol. i. p. 338.

argument, we ought to substitute " the number of all finite numbers " for " the number of all numbers " ; we then obtain exactly the illustration given by our two rows, one containing all the finite numbers, the other only the even finite numbers. It will be seen that Leibniz regards it as self-contradictory to maintain that the whole is not greater than its part. But the word " greater " is one which is capable of many meanings ; for our purpose, we must substitute the less ambiguous phrase " containing a greater number of terms." In this sense, it is not self-contradictory for whole and part to be equal ; it is the realization of this fact which has made the modern theory of infinity possible.

There is an interesting discussion of the reflexiveness of infinite wholes in the first of Galileo's Dialogues on Motion. I quote from a translation published in 1730.[1] The personages in the dialogue are Salviati, Sagredo, and Simplicius, and they reason as follows :

" *Simp.* Here already arises a Doubt which I think is not to be resolv'd ; and that is this : Since 'tis plain that one Line is given greater than another, and since both contain infinite Points, we must surely necessarily infer, that we have found in the same Species something greater than Infinite, since the Infinity of Points of the greater Line exceeds the Infinity of Points of the lesser. But now, to assign an Infinite greater than an Infinite, is what I can't possibly conceive.

[1] *Mathematical Discourses concerning two new sciences relating to mechanics and local motion, in four dialogues.* By Galileo Galilei, Chief Philosopher and Mathematician to the Grand Duke of Tuscany. Done into English from the Italian, by Tho. Weston, late Master, and now published by John Weston, present Master, of the Academy at Greenwich. See pp. 46 ff.

" *Salv.* These are some of those Difficulties which arise from Discourses which our finite Understanding makes about Infinites, by ascribing to them Attributes which we give to Things finite and terminate, which I think most improper, because those Attributes of Majority, Minority, and Equality, agree not with Infinities, of which we can't say that one is greater than, less than, or equal to another. For Proof whereof I have something come into my Head, which (that I may be the better understood) I will propose by way of Interrogatories to *Simplicius*, who started this Difficulty. To begin then : I suppose you know which are square Numbers, and which not ?

" *Simp.* I know very well that a square Number is that which arises from the Multiplication of any Number into itself ; thus 4 and 9 are square Numbers, that arising from 2, and this from 3, multiplied by themselves.

" *Salv.* Very well ; And you also know, that as the Products are call'd Squares, the Factors are call'd Roots : And that the other Numbers, which proceed not from Numbers multiplied into themselves, are not Squares. Whence taking in all Numbers, both Squares and Not Squares, if I should say, that the Not Squares are more than the Squares, should I not be in the right ?

" *Simp.* Most certainly.

" *Salv.* If I go on with you then, and ask you, How many squar'd Numbers there are ? you may truly answer, That there are as many as are their proper Roots, since every Square has its own Root, and every Root its own Square, and since no Square has more than one Root, nor any Root more than one Square.

" *Simp.* Very true.

" *Salv.* But now, if I should ask how many Roots there are, you can't deny but there are as many as there are Numbers, since there's no Number but what's the Root to some Square. And this being granted, we may likewise affirm, that there are as many square Numbers, as there are Numbers ; for there are as many Squares as there are Roots, and as many Roots as Numbers. And yet in the Beginning of this, we said, there were many more Numbers than Squares, the greater Part of Numbers being not Squares : And tho' the Number of Squares decreases in a greater proportion, as we go on to bigger Numbers, for count to an Hundred you'll find 10 Squares, viz. 1, 4, 9, 16, 25, 36, 49, 64, 81, 100, which is the same as to say the 10th Part are Squares ; in Ten thousand only the 100th Part are Squares ; in a Million only the 1000th : And yet in an infinite Number, if we can but comprehend it, we may say the Squares are as many as all the Numbers taken together.

" *Sagr.* What must be determin'd then in this Case ?

" *Salv.* I see no other way, but by saying that all Numbers are infinite ; Squares are Infinite, their Roots Infinite, and that the Number of Squares is not less than the Number of Numbers, nor this less than that : and then by concluding that the Attributes or Terms of Equality, Majority, and Minority, have no Place in Infinites, but are confin'd to terminate Quantities."

The way in which the problem is expounded in the above discussion is worthy of Galileo, but the solution suggested is not the right one. It is actually the case that the number of square (finite) numbers is the same as the number of (finite) numbers. The fact that, so long as we confine ourselves to numbers less than some given finite number, the proportion of squares tends towards zero as the given finite number increases, does not contradict the fact that the number of all finite squares is the same as the number of all finite numbers. This is only an instance of the fact, now familiar to mathematicians, that the *limit* of a function as the variable *approaches* a given point may not be the same as its *value* when the variable actually *reaches* the given point. But although the infinite numbers which Galileo discusses are equal, Cantor has shown that what Simplicius could not conceive is true, namely that there are an infinite number of different infinite numbers, and that the conception of *greater* and *less* can be perfectly well applied to them. The whole of Simplicius's difficulty comes, as is evident, from his belief that, if *greater* and *less* can be applied, a part of an infinite collection must have fewer terms than the whole ; and when this is denied, all contradictions disappear. As regards greater and less lengths of lines, which is the problem from which the above discussion starts, that involves a meaning of *greater* and *less* which is not arithmetical. The number of points is the same in a long line and in a short one, being in fact the same as the number of points in all space. The *greater* and *less* of metrical geometry involves the new metrical conception of *congruence*, which cannot be developed out of arithmetical considerations alone. But this question has not the fundamental importance which belongs to the arithmetical theory of infinity.

(2) *Non-inductiveness.*—The second property by which infinite numbers are distinguished from finite numbers is the property of non-inductiveness. This will be best explained by defining the positive property of inductiveness which characterizes the finite numbers,

and which is named after the method of proof known as " mathematical induction."

Let us first consider what is meant by calling a property " hereditary " in a given series. Take such a property as being named Jones. If a man is named Jones, so is his son ; we will therefore call the property of being called Jones hereditary with respect to the relation of father and son. If a man is called Jones, all his descendants in the direct male line are called Jones ; this follows from the fact that the property is hereditary. Now, instead of the relation of father and son, consider the relation of a finite number to its immediate successor, that is, the relation which holds between 0 and 1, between 1 and 2, between 2 and 3, and so on. If a property of numbers is hereditary with respect to this relation, then if it belongs to (say) 100, it must belong also to all finite numbers greater than 100 ; for, being hereditary, it belongs to 101 because it belongs to 100, and it belongs to 102 because it belongs to 101, and so on—where the " and so on " will take us, sooner or later, to any finite number greater than 100. Thus, for example, the property of being greater than 99 is hereditary in the series of finite numbers ; and generally, a property is hereditary in this series when, given any number that possesses the property, the next number must always also possess it.

It will be seen that a hereditary property, though it must belong to all the finite numbers greater than a given number possessing the property, need not belong to all the numbers less than this number. For example, the hereditary property of being greater than 99 belongs to 100 and all greater numbers, but not to any smaller number. Similarly, the hereditary property of being called Jones belongs to all the descendants (in the direct male line) of those who have this property, but not to all their ancestors, because we reach at last a first Jones, before whom the ancestors have no surname. It is obvious, however, that any hereditary property possessed by Adam must belong to all men ; and similarly any hereditary property possessed by o must belong to all finite numbers. This is the principle of what is called " mathematical induction." It frequently happens, when we wish to prove that all finite numbers have some property, that we have first to prove that o has the property, and then that the property is hereditary, i.e. that, if it belongs to a given number, then it belongs to the next number. Owing to the fact that such proofs are called " inductive," I shall call the properties to which they are applicable " inductive" properties. Thus an inductive property of numbers is one which is hereditary and belongs to o.

Taking any one of the natural numbers, say 29, it is easy to see that it must have all inductive properties. For since such properties belong to o and are hereditary, they belong to 1 ; therefore, since they are hereditary, they belong to 2, and so on ; by twenty-nine repetitions of such arguments we show that they belong to 29. We may *define* the " inductive" numbers as *all those that possess all inductive properties* ; they will be the same as what are called the " natural" numbers, i.e. the ordinary finite whole numbers. To all such numbers, proofs by mathematical induction can be validly applied. They are those numbers, we may loosely say, which can be reached from o by successive additions of 1 ; in other words, they are all the numbers that can be reached by counting.

But beyond all these numbers, there are the infinite numbers, and infinite numbers do not have all inductive properties. Such numbers, therefore, may be called non-inductive. All those properties of numbers which are proved by an imaginary step-by-step process from one number to the next are liable to fail when we come to infinite numbers. The first of the infinite numbers has no immediate predecessor, because there is no greatest finite number ; thus no succession of steps from one number to the next will ever reach from a finite number to an infinite one, and the step-by-step method of proof fails. This is another reason for the supposed self contradictions of infinite number. Many of the most familiar properties of numbers, which custom had led people to regard as logically necessary, are in fact only demonstrable by the step-by-step method, and fail to be true of infinite numbers. But so soon as we realize the necessity of proving such properties by mathematical induction, and the strictly limited scope of this method of proof, the supposed contradictions are seen to contradict, not logic, but only our prejudices and mental habits.

The property of being increased by the addition of 1—i.e. the property of non-reflexiveness—may serve to illustrate the limitations of mathematical induction. It is easy to prove that 0 is increased by the addition of 1, and that, if a given number is increased by the addition of 1, so is the next number, i.e. the number obtained by the addition of 1. It follows that each of the natural numbers is increased by the addition of 1. This follows generally from the general argument, and follows for each particular case by a sufficient number of applications of the argument. We first prove that 0 is not equal to 1 ; then, since the property of being increased by 1 is hereditary, it follows that 1 is not equal to 2 ; hence it follows that 2 is not equal to 3 ; if we wish to prove that 30,000 is not equal to

30,001, we can do so by repeating this reasoning 30,000 times. But we cannot prove in this way that *all* numbers are increased by the addition of 1; we can only prove that this holds of the numbers attainable by successive additions of 1 starting from 0. The reflexive numbers, which lie beyond all those attainable in this way, are as a matter of fact not increased by the addition of 1.

The two properties of reflexiveness and non-inductiveness, which we have considered as characteristics of infinite numbers, have not so far been proved to be always found together. It is known that all reflexive numbers are non-inductive, but it is not known that all non-inductive numbers are reflexive. Fallacious proofs of this proposition have been published by many writers, including myself, but up to the present no valid proof has been discovered. The infinite numbers actually known, however, are all reflexive as well as non-inductive; thus, in mathematical practice, if not in theory, the two properties are always associated. For our purposes, therefore, it will be convenient to ignore the bare possibility that there may be non-inductive non-reflexive numbers, since all known numbers are either inductive or reflexive.

When infinite numbers are first introduced to people, they are apt to refuse the name of numbers to them, because their behaviour is so different from that of finite numbers that it seems a wilful misuse of terms to call them numbers at all. In order to meet this feeling, we must now turn to the logical basis of arithmetic, and consider the logical definition of numbers.

The logical definition of numbers, though it seems an essential support to the theory of infinite numbers, was in fact discovered independently and by a different man. The theory of infinite numbers—that is to say, the arithmetical as opposed to the logical part of the theory—was discovered by Georg Cantor, and published by him in 1882–3.[1] The definition of number was discovered about the same time by a man whose great genius has not received the recognition it deserves —I mean Gottlob Frege of Jena. His first work, *Begriffsschrift*, published in 1879, contained the very important theory of hereditary properties in a series to which I alluded in connection with inductiveness. His definition of number is conitaned in his second work, published in 1884, and entitled *Die Grundlagen der Arithmetik, eine logisch-mathematische Untersuchung über den Begriff der Zahl*.[2] It is with this book that the logical theory of arithmetic begins, and it will repay us to consider Frege's analysis in some detail.

Frege begins by noting the increased desire for logical strictness in mathematical demonstrations which distinguishes modern mathematicians from their predecessors, and points out that this must lead to a critical investigation of the definition of number. He proceeds to show the inadequacy of previous philosophical theories, especially of the " synthetic *a priori* " theory of Kant and the empirical theory of Mill. This brings him to the question : What kind of object is it that number can properly be ascribed to ? He points out that physical things may be regarded as one or many : for example, if a tree has a thousand leaves, they may be taken altogether as constituting its

---

[1] In his *Grundlagen einer allgemeinen Mannichfaltigkeitslehre* and in articles in *Acta Mathematica*, vol. ii.

[2] The definition of number contained in this book, and elaborated in the *Grundgesetze der Arithmetik* (vol. i., 1893 ; vol. ii., 1903), was rediscovered by me in ignorance of Frege's work. I wish to state as emphatically as possible—what seems still often ignored—that his discovery antedated mine by eighteen years.

foliage, which would count as one, not as a thousand ; and *one* pair of boots is the same object as *two* boots. It follows that physical things are not the subjects of which number is properly predicated ; for when we have discovered the proper subjects, the number to be ascribed must be unambiguous. This leads to a discussion of the very prevalent view that number is really something psychological and subjective, a view which Frege emphatically rejects. " Number," he says, " is as little an object of psychology or an outcome of psychical processes as the North Sea. . . . The botanist wishes to state something which is just as much a fact when he gives the number of petals in a flower as when he gives its colour. The one depends as little as the other upon our caprice. There is therefore a certain similarity between number and colour ; but this does not consist in the fact that both are sensibly perceptible in external things, but in the fact that both are objective " (p. 34).

" I distinguish the objective," he continues, " from the palpable, the spatial, the actual. The earth's axis, the centre of mass of the solar system, are objective, but I should not call them actual, like the earth itself " (p. 35). He concludes that number is neither spatial and physical, nor subjective, but non-sensible and objective. This conclusion is important, since it applies to all the subject-matter of mathematics and logic. Most philosophers have thought that the physical and the mental between them exhausted the world of being. Some have argued that the objects of mathematics were obviously not subjective, and therefore must be physical and empirical ; others have argued that they were obviously not physical, and therefore must be subjective and mental. Both sides were right in what they denied, and wrong in what they asserted ; Frege has the merit of accepting both denials, and finding a third assertion by recognizing the world of logic, which is neither mental nor physical.

The fact is, as Frege points out, that no number, not even 1, is applicable to physical things, but only to general terms or descriptions, such as " man," " satellite of the earth," " satellite of Venus." The general term " man " is applicable to a certain number of objects : there are in the world so and so many men. The unity which philosophers rightly feel to be necessary for the assertion of a number is the unity of the general term, and it is the general term which is the proper subject of number. And this applies equally when there is one object or none which falls under the general term. " Satellite of the earth " is a term only applicable to one object, namely, the moon. But " one " is not a property of the moon itself, which may equally well be regarded as many molecules : it is a property of the general term " earth's satellite." Similarly, 0 is a property of the general term " satellite of Venus," because Venus has no satellite. Here at last we have an intelligible theory of the number 0. This was impossible if numbers applied to physical objects, because obviously no physical object could have the number 0. Thus, in seeking our definition of number we have arrived so far at the result that numbers are properties of general terms or general descriptions, not of physical things or of mental occurrences.

Instead of speaking of a general term, such as " man," as the subject of which a number can be asserted, we may, without making any serious change, take the subject as the class or collection of objects— i.e. " mankind " in the above instance—to which the general term in question is applicable. Two general

terms, such as " man " and " featherless biped,"
which are applicable to the same collection of objects,
will obviously have the same number of instances ;
thus the number depends upon the class, not upon
the selection of this or that general term to describe
it, provided several general terms can be found to
describe the same class. But some general term is
always necessary in order to describe a class. Even
when the terms are enumerated, as " this and that
and the other," the collection is constituted by the
general property of being either this, or that, or the
other, and only so acquires the unity which enables
us to speak of it as *one* collection. And in the case
of an infinite class, enumeration is impossible, so that
description by a general characteristic common and
peculiar to the members of the class is the only possible
description. Here, as we see, the theory of number to
which Frege was led by purely logical considerations
becomes of use in showing how infinite classes can be
amenable to number in spite of being incapable of
enumeration.

Frege next asks the question : When do two collections
have the same number of terms ? In ordinary life,
we decide this question by counting ; but counting,
as we saw, is impossible in the case of infinite collections,
and is not logically fundamental with finite collections.
We want, therefore, a different method of answering
our question. An illustration may help to make the
method clear. I do not know how many married
men there are in England, but I do know that the
number is the same as the number of married women.
The reason I know this is that the relation of husband
and wife relates one man to one woman and one woman
to one man. A relation of this sort is called a one-
one relation. The relation of father to son is called a

one-many relation, because a man can have only one father but may have many sons ; conversely, the relation of son to father is called a many-one relation. But the relation of husband to wife (in Christian countries) is called one-one, because a man cannot have more than one wife, or a woman more than one husband. Now, whenever there is a one-one relation between all the terms of one collection and all the terms of another severally, as in the case of English husbands and English wives, the number of terms in the one collection is the same as the number in the other ; but when there is not such a relation, the number is different. This is the answer to the question : When do two collections have the same number of terms ?

We can now at last answer the question : What is meant by the number of terms in a given collection ? When there is a one-one relation between all the terms of one collection and all the terms of another severally, we shall say that the two collections are " similar." We have just seen that two similar collections have the same number of terms. This leads us to define the number of a given collection as the class of all collections that are similar to it ; that is to say, we set up the following formal definition :

" The number of terms in a given class " is defined as meaning " the class of all classes that are similar to the given class."

This definition, as Frege (expressing it in slightly different terms) showed, yields the usual arithmetical properties of numbers. It is applicable equally to finite and infinite numbers, and it does not require the admission of some new and mysterious set of metaphysical entities. It shows that it is not physical objects, but classes or the general terms by which they are defined, of which numbers can be asserted ; and it applies to 0 and 1 without any of the difficulties which other theories find in dealing with these two special cases.

The above definition is sure to produce, at first sight, a feeling of oddity, which is liable to cause a certain dissatisfaction. It defines the number 2, for instance, as the class of all couples, and the number 3 as the class of all triads. This does not *seem* to be what we have hitherto been meaning when we spoke of 2 and 3, though it would be difficult to say *what* we had been meaning. The answer to a feeling cannot be a logical argument, but nevertheless the answer in this case is not without importance. In the first place, it will be found that when an idea which has grown familiar as an unanalysed whole is first resolved accurately into its component parts—which is what we do when we define it—there is almost always a feeling of un-familiarity produced by the analysis, which tends to cause a protest against the definition. In the second place, it may be admitted that the definition, like all definitions, is to a certain extent arbitrary. In the case of the small finite numbers, such as 2 and 3, it would be possible to frame definitions more nearly in accordance with our unanalysed feeling of what we mean ; but the method of such definitions would lack uniformity, and would be found to fail sooner or later— at latest when we reached infinite numbers.

In the third place, the real desideratum about such a definition as that of number is not that it should represent as nearly as possible the ideas of those who have not gone through the analysis required in order to reach a definition, but that it should give us objects having the requisite properties. Numbers, in fact, must satisfy the formulæ of arithmetic ; any indubitable set of objects fulfilling this requirement may be called numbers. So far, the simplest set known to fulfil this requirement is the set introduced by the above definition. In comparison with this merit, the question whether the objects to which the definition applies are like or unlike the vague ideas of numbers entertained by those who cannot give a definition, is one of very little importance. All the important requirements are fulfilled by the above definition, and the sense of oddity which is at first unavoidable will be found to wear off very quickly with the growth of familiarity.

There is, however, a certain logical doctrine which may be thought to form an objection to the above definition of numbers as classes of classes—I mean the doctrine that there are no such objects as classes at all. It might be thought that this doctrine would make havoc of a theory which reduces numbers to classes, and of the many other theories in which we have made use of classes. This, however, would be a mistake : none of these theories are any the worse for the doctrine that classes are fictions. What the doctrine is, and why it is not destructive, I will try briefly to explain.

On account of certain rather complicated difficulties, culminating in definite contradictions, I was led to the view that nothing that can be said significantly about things, i.e. particulars, can be said significantly (i.e. either truly or falsely) about classes of things. That is to say, if, in any sentence in which a thing is mentioned, you substitute a class for the thing, you no longer have a sentence that has any meaning : the sentence is no longer either true or false, but a meaningless collection of words. Appearances to the contrary can be dispelled by a moment's reflection. For

example, in the sentence, " Adam is fond of apples,"
you may substitute *mankind*, and say, " Mankind is
fond of apples." But obviously you do not mean
that there is one individual, called " mankind," which
munches apples : you mean that the separate individuals who compose mankind are each severally fond
of apples.

Now, if nothing that can be said significantly about
a thing can be said significantly about a class of things,
it follows that classes of things cannot have the same
kind of reality as things have ; for if they had, a class
could be substituted for a thing in a proposition
predicating the kind of reality which would be common
to both. This view is really consonant to common
sense. In the third or fourth century B.C. there lived
a Chinese philosopher named Hui Tzŭ, who maintained
that " a bay horse and a dun cow are three ; because
taken separately they are two, and taken together
they are one : two and one make three." [1] The
author from whom I quote says that Hui Tzŭ " was
particularly fond of the quibbles which so delighted
the sophists or unsound reasoners of ancient Greece,"
and this no doubt represents the judgment of common
sense upon such arguments. Yet if collections of
things were things, his contention would be irrefragable. It is only because the bay horse and the dun
cow taken together are not a new thing that we can
escape the conclusion that there are three things
wherever there are two.

When it is admitted that classes are not things, the
question arises : What do we mean by statements
which are nominally about classes ? Take such a
statement as, " The class of people interested in

[1] Giles, *The Civilisation of China* (Home University Library),
p. 147.

mathematical logic is not very numerous." Obviously this reduces itself to, " Not very many people are interested in mathematical logic." For the sake of definiteness, let us substitute some particular number, say 3, for " very many." Then our statement is, " Not three people are interested in mathematical logic." This may be expressed in the form : " If x is interested in mathematical logic, and also y is interested, and also z is interested, then x is identical with y, or x is identical with z, or y is identical with z." Here there is no longer any reference at all to a " class." In some such way, all statements nominally about a class can be reduced to statements about what follows from the hypothesis of anything's having the defining property of the class. All that is wanted, therefore, in order to render the *verbal* use of classes legitimate, is a uniform method of interpreting propositions in which such a use occurs, so as to obtain propositions in which there is no longer any such use. The definition of such a method is a technical matter, which Dr. Whitehead and I have dealt with elsewhere, and which we need not enter into on this occasion.[1]

If the theory that classes are merely symbolic is accepted, it follows that numbers are not actual entities, but that propositions in which numbers verbally occur have not really any constituents corresponding to numbers, but only a certain logical form which is not a part of propositions having this form. This is in fact the case with all the apparent objects of logic and mathematics. Such words as *or, not, if, there is, identity, greater, plus, nothing, everything, function*, and so on, are not names of definite objects, like " John " or " Jones," but are words which require

---

[1] Cf. *Principia Mathematica*, § 20, and Introduction, chapter iii.

a context in order to have meaning. All of them are *formal*, that is to say, their occurrence indicates a certain form of proposition, not a certain constituent. " Logical constants," in short, are not entities ; the words expressing them are not names, and cannot significantly be made into logical subjects except when it is the words themselves, as opposed to their meanings, that are being discussed.[1] This fact has a very important bearing on all logic and philosophy, since it shows how they differ from the special sciences. But the questions raised are so large and so difficult that it is impossible to pursue them further on this occasion.

[1] See *Tractatus Logico-Philosophicus*, by Ludwig Wittgenstein (Kegan Paul, 1922).

LECTURE VIII

ON THE NOTION OF CAUSE, WITH APPLICA-
TIONS TO THE FREE-WILL PROBLEM

THE nature of philosophic analysis, as illustrated in our previous lectures, can now be stated in general terms. We start from a body of common knowledge, which constitutes our data. On examination, the data are found to be complex, rather vague, and largely interdependent logically. By analysis we reduce them to propositions which are as nearly as possible simple and precise, and we arrange them in deductive chains, in which a certain number of initial propositions form a logical guarantee for all the rest. These initial propositions are *premisses* for the body of knowledge in question. Premisses are thus quite different from data—they are simpler, more precise, and less infected with logical redundancy. If the work of analysis has been performed completely, they will be wholly free from logical redundancy, wholly precise, and as simple as is logically compatible with their leading to the given body of knowledge. The discovery of these premisses belongs to philosophy ; but the work of deducing the body of common knowledge from them belongs to mathematics, if " mathematics " is interpreted in a somewhat liberal sense.

But besides the logical analysis of the common knowledge which forms our data, there is the consideration of its degree of certainty. When we have arrived at its premisses, we may find that some of them seem open to doubt, and we may find further that this doubt extends to those of our original data which depend upon these doubtful premisses. In our third lecture, for example, we saw that the part of physics which depends upon testimony, and thus upon the existence of other minds than our own, does not seem so certain as the part which depends exclusively upon our own sense-data and the laws of logic. Similarly, it used to be felt that the parts of geometry which depend upon the axiom of parallels have less certainty than the parts which are independent of this premiss. We may say, generally, that what commonly passes as knowledge is not all equally certain, and that, when analysis into premisses has been effected, the degree of certainty of any consequence of the premisses will depend upon that of the most doubtful premiss employed in proving this consequence. Thus analysis into premisses serves not only a logical purpose, but also the purpose of facilitating an estimate as to the degree of certainty to be attached to this or that derivative belief. In view of the fallibility of all human beliefs, this service seems at least as important as the purely logical services rendered by philosophical analysis.

In the present lecture, I wish to apply the analytic method to the notion of " cause," and to illustrate the discussion by applying it to the problem of free will. For this purpose I shall inquire : I, what is meant by a causal law ; II, what is the evidence that causal laws have held hitherto ; III, what is the evidence that they will continue to hold in the future ; IV, how the causality which is used in science differs from that of common sense and traditional philosophy ;

V, what new light is thrown on the question of free will by our analysis of the notion of " cause."

I. By a " causal law " I mean any general proposition in virtue of which it is possible to infer the existence of one thing or event from the existence of another or of a number of others. If you hear thunder without having seen lightning, you infer that there nevertheless was a flash, because of the general proposition, " All thunder is preceded by lightning." When Robinson Crusoe sees a footprint, he infers a human being, and he might justify his inference by the general proposition, " All marks in the ground shaped like a human foot are subsequent to a human being's standing where the marks are." When we see the sun set, we expect that it will rise again the next day. When we hear a man speaking, we infer that he has certain thoughts. All these inferences are due to causal laws.

A causal law, we said, allows us to infer the existence of one *thing* (or *event*) from the existence of one or more others. The word " thing " here is to be understood as only applying to particulars, i.e. as excluding such logical objects as numbers or classes or abstract properties and relations, and including sense-data, with whatever is logically of the same type as sense-data.[1] In so far as a causal law is directly verifiable, the thing inferred and the thing from which it is inferred must both be data, though they need not both be data at the same time. In fact, a causal law which is being used to extend our knowledge of existence must be applied to what, at the moment, is not a datum ; it is in the possibility of such application

---

[1] Thus we are not using "thing" here in the sense of a class of correlated "aspects," as we did in Lecture III. Each "aspect" will count separately in stating causal laws.

that the practical utility of a causal law consists. The important point, for our present purpose, however, is that what is inferred is a " thing," a " particular," an object having the kind of reality that belongs to objects of sense, not an abstract object such as virtue or the square root of two.

But we cannot become acquainted with a particular except by its being actually given. Hence the particular inferred by a causal law must be only *described* with more or less exactness ; it cannot be *named* until the inference is verified. Moreover, since the causal law is *general*, and capable of applying to many cases, the given particular from which we infer must allow the inference in virtue of some general characteristic, not in virtue of its being just the particular that it is. This is obvious in all our previous instances : we infer the unperceived lightning from the thunder, not in virtue of any peculiarity of the thunder, but in virtue of its resemblance to other claps of thunder. Thus a causal law must state that the existence of a thing of a certain sort (or of a number of things of a number of assigned sorts) implies the existence of another thing having a relation to the first which remains invariable so long as the first is of the kind in question.

It is to be observed that what is constant in a causal law is not the object or objects given, nor yet the object inferred, both of which may vary within wide limits, but the *relation* between what is given and what is inferred. The principle, " same cause, same effect," which is sometimes said to be the principle of causality, is much narrower in its scope than the principle which really occurs in science ; indeed, if strictly interpreted, it has no scope at all, since the " same " cause never recurs exactly. We shall return to this point at a later stage of the discussion.

The particular which is inferred may be uniquely determined by the causal law, or may be only described in such general terms that many different particulars might satisfy the description. This depends upon whether the constant relation affirmed by the causal law is one which only one term can have to the data, or one which many terms may have. If many terms may have the relation in question, science will not be satisfied until it has found some more stringent law, which will enable us to determine the inferred things uniquely.

Since all known things are in time, a causal law must take account of temporal relations. It will be part of the causal law to state a relation of succession or coexistence between the thing given and the thing inferred. When we hear thunder and infer that there was lightning, the law states that the thing inferred is earlier than the thing given. Conversely, when we see lightning and wait expectantly for the thunder, the law states that the thing given is earlier than the thing inferred. When we infer a man's thoughts from his words, the law states that the two are (at least approximately) simultaneous.

If a causal law is to achieve the precision at which science aims, it must not be content with a vague *earlier* or *later*, but must state how much earlier or how much later. That is to say, the time-relation between the thing given and the thing inferred ought to be capable of exact statement ; and usually the inference to be drawn is different according to the length and direction of the interval. " A quarter of an hour ago this man was alive ; **an** hour hence he will be cold." Such a statement involves two causal laws, one inferring from a datum something which existed a quarter of an hour ago, the other inferring from the same datum something which will exist an hour hence.

Often a causal law involved not one datum, but many, which need not be all simultaneous with each other, though their time-relations must be given. The general scheme of a causal law will be as follows :

" Whenever things occur in certain relations to each other (among which their time-relations must be included), then a thing having a fixed relation to these things will occur at a date fixed relatively to their dates."

The things given will not, in practice, be things that only exist for an instant, for such things, if there are any, can never be data. The things given will each occupy some finite time. They may be not static things, but processes, especially motions. We have considered in an earlier lecture the sense in which a motion may be a datum, and need not now recur to this topic.

It is not essential to a causal law that the object inferred should be later than some or all of the data. It may equally well be earlier or at the same time. The only thing essential is that the law should be such as to enable us to infer the existence of an object which we can more or less accurately describe in terms of the data.

II. I come now to our second question, namely : What is the nature of the evidence that causal laws have held hitherto, at least in the observed portions of the past ? This question must not be confused with the further question : Does this evidence warrant us in assuming the truth of causal laws in the future and in unobserved portions of the past ? For the present, I am only asking what are the grounds which lead to a belief in causal laws, not whether these grounds are adequate to support the belief in universal causation.

The first step is the discovery of approximate un-analysed uniformities of sequence or coexistence. After lightning comes thunder, after a blow received comes pain, after approaching a fire comes warmth ; again, there are uniformities of coexistence, for ex-ample between touch and sight, between certain sensations in the throat and the sound of one's own voice, and so on. Every such uniformity of sequence or coexistence, after it has been experienced a certain number of times, is followed by an expectation that it will be repeated on future occasions, i.e. that where one of the correlated events is found, the other will be found also. The connection of experienced past uniformity with expectation as to the future is just one of those uniformities of sequence which we have observed to be true hitherto. This affords a psycho-logical account of what may be called the animal belief in causation, because it is something which can be observed in horses and dogs, and is rather a habit of acting than a real belief. So far, we have merely repeated Hume, who carried the discussion of cause up to this point, but did not, apparently, perceive how much remained to be said.

Is there, in fact, any characteristic, such as might be called causality or uniformity, which is found to hold throughout the observed past ? And if so, how is it to be stated ?

The particular uniformities which we mentioned before, such as lightning being followed by thunder, are not found to be free from exceptions. We some-times see lightning without hearing thunder ; and although, in such a case, we suppose that thunder might have been heard if we had been nearer to the lightning, that is a supposition based on theory, and therefore incapable of being invoked to support the theory. What does seem, however, to be shown by scientific experience is this : that where an observed uniformity fails, some wider uniformity can be found, embracing more circumstances, and subsuming both the successes and the failures of the previous uniformity. Unsupported bodies in air fall, unless they are balloons or aeroplanes; but the principles of mechanics give uniformities which apply to balloons and aeroplanes just as accurately as to bodies that fall. There is much that is hypothetical and more or less artificial in the uniformities affirmed by mechanics, because, when they cannot otherwise be made applicable, unobserved bodies are inferred in order to account for observed peculiarities. Still, it is an empirical fact that it is possible to preserve the laws by assuming such bodies, and that they never have to be assumed in circumstances in which they ought to be observable. Thus the empirical verification of mechanical laws may be admitted, although we must also admit that it is less complete and triumphant than is sometimes supposed.

Assuming now, what must be admitted to be doubtful, that the whole of the past has proceeded according to invariable laws, what can we say as to the nature of these laws ? They will not be of the simple type which asserts that the same cause always produces the same effect. We may take the law of gravitation as a sample of the kind of law that appears to be verified without exception. In order to state this law in a form which observation can confirm, we will confine it to the solar system. It then states that the motions of planets and their satellites have at every instant an acceleration compounded of accelerations towards all the other bodies in the solar system, proportional to the matters of these bodies and inversely proportional to the squares of their distances. In virtue of this law, given the state of the solar system throughout any finite time, however short, its state at all earlier and later times is determinate except in so far as other forces than gravitation or other bodies than those in the solar system have to be taken into consideration. But other forces, so far as science can discover, appear to be equally regular, and equally capable of being summed up in single causal laws. If the mechanical account of matter were complete, the whole physical history of the universe, past and future, could be inferred from a sufficient number of data concerning an assigned finite time, however short.

In the mental world, the evidence for the universality of causal laws is less complete than in the physical world. Psychology cannot boast of any triumph comparable to gravitational astronomy. Nevertheless-the evidence is not very greatly less than in the physical world. The crude and approximate causal laws from which science starts are just as easy to discover in the mental sphere as in the physical. In the world of sense, there are to begin with the correlations of sight and touch and so on, and the facts which lead us to connect various kinds of sensations with eyes, ears, nose, tongue, etc. Then there are such facts as that our body moves in answer to our volitions. Exceptions exist, but are capable of being explained as easily as the exceptions to the rule that unsupported bodies in air fall. There is, in fact, just such a degree of evidence for causal laws in psychology as will warrant the psychologist in assuming them as a matter of course, though not such a degree as will suffice to remove all doubt from the mind of a sceptical inquirer. It should be observed that causal laws in which the given term is mental and the inferred term physical, or *vice versa*, are at least as easy to discover as causal laws in which both terms are mental.

It will be noticed that, although we have spoken of causal laws, we have not hitherto introduced the word " cause." At this stage, it will be well to say a few words on legitimate and illegitimate uses of this word. The word " cause," in the scientific account of the world, belongs only to the early stages, in which small preliminary, approximate generalizations are being ascertained with a view to subsequent larger and more invariable laws. We may say " Arsenic causes death," so long as we are ignorant of the precise process by which the result is brought about. But in a sufficiently advanced science, the word " cause " will not occur in any statement of invariable laws. There is, however, a somewhat rough and loose use of the word " cause " which may be preserved. The approximate uniformities which lead to its pre-scientific employment may turn out to be true in all but very rare and exceptional circumstances, perhaps in all circumstances that actually occur. In such cases, it is convenient to be able to speak of the antecedent event as the " cause " and the subsequent event as the " effect." In this sense, provided it is realized that the sequence is not necessary and may have exceptions, it is still possible to employ the words " cause " and " effect." It is in this sense, and in this sense only, that we shall intend the words when we speak of one particular event " causing " another particular event, as we must sometimes do if we are to avoid intolerable circumlocution.

III. We come now to our third question, namely :
What reason can be given for believing that causal
laws will hold in future, or that they have held in
unobserved portions of the past ?

What we have said so far is that there have been
hitherto certain observed causal laws, and that all the
empirical evidence we possess is compatible with the
view that everything, both mental and physical, so
far as our observation has extended, has happened in
accordance with causal laws. The law of universal
causation, suggested by these facts, may be enunciated
as follows :

" There are such invariable relations between different events at the same or different times that, given
the state of the whole universe throughout any finite
time, however short, every previous and subsequent
event can theoretically be determined as a function
of the given events during that time."

Have we any reason to believe this universal law ?
Or, to ask a more modest question, have we any
reason to believe that a particular causal law, such as
the law of gravitation, will continue to hold in the
future ?

Among observed causal laws is this, that observation
of uniformities is followed by expectation of their
recurrence. A horse who has been driven always
along a certain road expects to be driven along that
road again ; a dog who is always fed at a certain hour
expects food at that hour and not at any other. Such
expectations, as Hume pointed out, explain only too
well the common-sense belief in uniformities of sequence, but they afford absolutely no logical ground
for beliefs as to the future, not even for the belief
that we shall continue to expect the continuation of
experienced uniformities, for that is precisely one of

those causal laws for which a ground has to be sought. If Hume's account of causation is the last word, we have not only no reason to suppose that the sun will rise to-morrow, but no reason to suppose that five minutes hence we shall still expect it to rise to-morrow.

It may, of course, be said that all inferences as to the future are in fact invalid, and I do not see how such a view could be disproved. But, while admitting the legitimacy of such a view, we may nevertheless inquire : If inferences as to the future *are* valid, what principle must be involved in making them ?

The principle involved is the principle of induction,[1] which, if it is true, must be an *a priori* logical law, not capable of being proved or disproved by experience. It is a difficult question how this principle ought to be formulated ; but if it is to warrant the inferences which we wish to make by its means, it must lead to the following proposition : " If, in a great number of instances, a thing of a certain kind is associated in a certain way with a thing of a certain other kind, it is probable that a thing of the one kind is always similarly associated with a thing of the other kind ; and as the number of instances increases, the probability approaches indefinitely near to certainty." It may well be questioned whether this proposition is true ; but if we admit it, we can infer that any characteristic of the whole of the observed past is likely to apply to the future and to the unobserved past. This proposition, therefore, if it is true, will warrant the inference that causal laws probably hold at all times, future as well as past ; but without this principle, the observed cases of the truth of causal laws afford

[1] On this subject, see Keynes's *Treatise on Probability* (Macmillan, 1921).

no presumption as to the unobserved cases, and therefore the existence of a thing not directly observed can never be validly inferred.

It is thus the principle of induction, rather than the law of causality, which is at the bottom of all inferences as to the existence of things not immediately given. With the principle of induction, all that is wanted for such inferences can be proved ; without it, all such inferences are invalid. This principle has not received the attention which its great importance deserves. Those who were interested in deductive logic naturally enough ignored it, while those who emphasized the scope of induction wished to maintain that all logic is empirical, and therefore could not be expected to realize that induction itself, their own darling, required a logical principle which obviously could not be proved inductively, and must therefore be *a priori* if it could be known at all.

The view that the law of causality itself is *a priori* cannot, I think, be maintained by anyone who realizes what a complicated principle it is. In the form which states that " every event has a cause " it looks simple ; but on examination, " cause " is merged in " causal law," and the definition of a " causal law " is found to be far from simple. There must necessarily be *some a priori* principle involved in inference from the existence of one thing to that of another, if such inference is ever valid ; but it would appear from the above analysis that the principle in question is induction, not causality. Whether inferences from past to future are valid depends wholly if our discussion has been sound, upon the inductive principle : if it is true, such inferences are valid, and if it is false, they are invalid.

IV. I come now to the question how the conception

of causal laws which we have arrived at is related to the traditional conception of cause as it occurs in philosophy and common sense.

Historically, the notion of cause has been bound up with that of human volition. The typical cause would be the fiat of a king. The cause is supposed to be " active," the effect " passive." From this it is easy to pass on to the suggestion that a " true " cause must contain some prevision of the effect ; hence the effect becomes the " end " at which the cause aims, and teleology replaces causation in the explanation of nature. But all such ideas, as applied to physics, are mere anthropomorphic superstitions. It is as a reaction against these errors that Mach and others have urged a purely " descriptive " view of physics : physics, they say, does not aim at telling us " why " things happen, but only " how " they happen. And if the question " why ? " means anything more than the search for a general law according to which a phenomenon occurs, then it is certainly the case that this question cannot be answered in physics and ought not to be asked. In this sense, the descriptive view is indubitably in the right. But in using causal laws to support inferences from the observed to the unobserved, physics ceases to be *purely* descriptive, and it is these laws which give the scientifically useful part of the traditional notion of " cause." There is therefore *something* to preserve in this notion, though it is a very tiny part of what is commonly assumed in orthodox metaphysics.

In order to understand the difference between the kind of cause which science uses and the kind which we naturally imagine, it is necessary to shut out, by an effort, everything that differentiates between past and future. This is an extraordinarily difficult thing to do, because our mental life is so intimately bound up with difference Not only do memory and hope make a difference in our feelings as regards past and future, but almost our whole vocabulary is filled with the idea of activity, of things done now for the sake of their future effects. All transitive verbs involve the notion of cause as activity, and would have to be replaced by some cumbrous periphrasis before this notion could be eliminated.

Consider such a statement as, " Brutus killed Cæsar." On another occasion, Brutus and Cæsar might engage our attention, but for the present it is the killing that we have to study. We may say that to kill a person is to cause his death intentionally. This means that desire for a person's death causes a certain act, because it is believed that that act will cause the person's death ; or more accurately, the desire and the belief jointly cause the act. Brutus desires that Cæsar should be dead, and believes that he will be dead if he is stabbed ; Brutus therefore stabs him, and the stab causes Cæsar's death, as Brutus expected it would. Every act which realizes a purpose involves two causal steps in this way : C is desired, and it is believed (truly if the purpose is achieved) that B will cause C ; the desire and the belief together cause B, which in turn causes C. Thus we have first A, which is a desire for C and a belief that B (an act) will cause C ; then we have B, the act caused by A, and believed to be a cause of C ; then, if the belief was correct, we have C, caused by B, and if the belief was incorrect we have disappointment. Regarded purely scientifically, this series A, B, C may equally well be considered in the inverse order, as they would be at a coroner's inquest. But from the point of view of Brutus, the desire, which comes at the beginning, is what makes the whole series interesting. We feel that if his desires had been different, the effects which he in fact produced would not have occurred. This is true, and gives him a sense of power and freedom. It is equally true that if the effects had not occurred, his desires would have been different, since being what they were the effects did occur. Thus the desires are determined by their consequences just as much as the consequences by the desires ; but as we cannot (in general) know in advance the consequences of our desires without knowing our desires, this form of inference is uninteresting as applied to our own acts, though quite vital as applied to those of others.

A cause, considered scientifically, has none of that analogy with volition which makes us imagine that the effect is *compelled* by it. A cause is an event or group of events of some known general character, and having a known relation to some other event, called the effect ; the relation being of such a kind that only one event, or at any rate only one well-defined sort of event, can have the relation to a given cause. It is customary only to give the name " effect " to an event which is later than the cause, but there is no kind of reason for this restriction. We shall do better to allow the effect to be before the cause or simultaneous with it, because nothing of any scientific importance depends upon its being after the cause.

If the inference from cause to effect is to be indubitable, it seems that the cause can hardly stop short of the whole universe. So long as anything is left out, something may be left out which alters the expected result. But for practical and scientific purposes, phenomena can be collected into groups which are causally self-contained, or nearly so. In the common notion of causation, the cause is a single event—we say the lightning causes the thunder, and so on. But it is difficult to know what we mean by a single event ; and it generally appears that, in order to have anything approaching certainty concerning the effect, it is necessary to include many more circumstances in the cause than unscientific common sense would suppose. But often a probable causal connection, where the cause is fairly simple, is of more practical importance than a more indubitable connection in which the cause is so complex as to be hard to ascertain.

To sum up : the strict, certain, universal law of causation which philosophers advocate is an ideal, possibly true, but not *known* to be true in virtue of any available evidence. What is actually known, as a matter of empirical science, is that certain constant relations are observed to hold between the members of a group of events at certain times, and that when such relations fail, as they sometimes do, it is usually possible to discover a new, more constant relation by enlarging the group. Any such constant relation between events of specified kinds with given intervals of time between them is a " causal law." But all causal laws are liable to exceptions, if the cause is less than the whole state of the universe ; we believe, on the basis of a good deal of experience, that such exceptions can be dealt with by enlarging the group we call the cause, but this belief, wherever it is still unverified, ought not .to be regarded as certain, but only as suggesting a direction for further inquiry.

A very common causal group consists of volitions and the consequent bodily acts, though exceptions arise (for example) through sudden paralysis. Another very frequent connection (though here the exceptions are much more numerous) is between a bodily act and the realization of the purpose which led to the act.

These connections are patent, whereas the causes of desires are more obscure. Thus it is natural to begin causal series with desires, to suppose that all causes are analogous to desires, and that desires themselves arise spontaneously. Such a view, however, is not one which any serious psychologist would maintain. But this brings us to the question of the application of our analysis of cause to the problem of free will.

V. The problem of free will is so intimately bound up with the analysis of causation that, old as it is, we need not despair of obtaining new light on it by the help of new views on the notion of cause. The free-will problem has, at one time or another, stirred men's passions profoundly, and the fear that the will might not be free has been to some men a source of great unhappiness. I believe that, under the influence of a cool analysis, the doubtful questions involved will be found to have no such emotional importance as is sometimes thought, since the disagreeable consequences supposed to flow from a denial of free will do not flow from this denial in any form in which there is reason to make it. It is not, however, on this account chiefly that I wish to discuss this problem, but rather because it affords a good example of the clarifying effect of analysis and of the interminable controversies which may result from its neglect.

Let us first try to discover what it is we really desire when we desire free will. Some of our reasons for desiring free will are profound, some trivial. To begin with the former : we do not wish to feel ourselves in the hands of fate, so that, however much we may desire to will one thing, we may nevertheless be compelled by an outside force to will another. We do not wish to think that, however much we may desire to act well, heredity and surroundings may force us into acting ill. We wish to feel that, in cases of doubt, our choice is momentous and lies within our power. Besides these desires, which are worthy of all respect, we have, however, others not so respectable, which equally make us desire free will. We do not like to think that other people, if they knew enough, could predict our actions, though we know that we can often predict those of other people, especially if they are elderly. Much as we esteem the old gentleman who is our neighbour in the country, we know that when grouse are mentioned he will tell the story of the grouse in the gun-room. But we ourselves are not so mechanical : we never tell an anecdote to the same person twice, or even once unless he is sure to enjoy it ; although we once met (say) Bismarck, we are quite capable of hearing him mentioned without relating the occasion when we met him. In this sense, everybody thinks that he himself has free will, though he knows that no one else has. The desire for this kind of free will seems to be no better than a form of vanity. I do not believe that this desire can be gratified with any certainty ; but the other, more respectable desires are, I believe, not inconsistent with any tenable form of determinism.

We have thus two questions to consider : (1) Are human actions theoretically predictable from a sufficient number of antecedents ? (2) Are human actions subject to an external compulsion ? The two questions, as I shall try to show, are entirely distinct, and we may answer the first in the affirmative without therefore being forced to give an affirmative answer to the second.

(1) *Are human actions theoretically predictable from a sufficient number of antecedents ?* Let us first endeavour to give precision to this question. We may

state the question thus : Is there some constant relation between an act and a certain number of earlier events, such that, when the earlier events are given, only one act, or at most only acts with some well-marked character, can have this relation to the earlier events ? If this is the case, then, as soon as the earlier events are known, it is theoretically possible to predict either the precise act, or at least the character necessary to its fulfilling the constant relation.

To this question, a negative answer has been given by Bergson, in a form which calls in question the general applicability of the law of causation. He maintains that every event, and more particularly every mental event, embodies so much of the past that it could not possibly have occurred at any earlier time, and is therefore necessarily quite different from all previous and subsequent events. If, for example, I read a certain poem many times, my experience on each occasion is modified by the previous readings, and my emotions are never repeated exactly. The principle of causation, according to him, asserts that the same cause, if repeated, will produce the same effect. But owing to memory, he contends, this principle does not apply to mental events. What is apparently the same cause, if repeated, is modified by the mere fact of repetition, and cannot produce the same effect. He infers that every mental event is a genuine novelty, not predictable from the past, because the past contains nothing exactly like it by which we could imagine it. And on this ground he regards the freedom of the will as unassailable.

Bergson's contention has undoubtedly a great deal of truth, and I have no wish to deny its importance. But I do not think its consequences are quite what he believes them to be. It is not necessary for the determinist to maintain that he can foresee the whole particularity of the act which will be performed. If he could foresee that A was going to murder B, his foresight would not be invalidated by the fact that he could not know all the infinite complexity of A's state of mind in committing the murder, nor whether the murder was to be performed with a knife or with a revolver. If the *kind* of act which will be performed can be foreseen within narrow limits, it is of little practical interest that there are fine shades which cannot be foreseen. No doubt every time the story of the grouse in the gun-room is told, there will be slight differences due to increasing habitualness, but they do not invalidate the prediction that the story will be told. And there is nothing in Bergson's argument to show that we can never predict what *kind* of act will be performed.

Again, his statement of the law of causation is inadequate. The law does not state merely that, if the *same* cause is repeated, the *same* effect will result. It states rather that there is a constant relation between causes of certain kinds and effects of certain kinds. For example, if a body falls freely, there is a constant relation between the height through which it falls and the time it takes in falling. It is not necessary to have a body fall through the *same* height which has been previously observed, in order to be able to foretell the length of time occupied in falling. If this were necessary, no prediction would be possible, since it would be impossible to make the height exactly the same on two occasions. Similarly, the attraction which the sun will exert on the earth is not only known at distances for which it has been observed, but at all distances, because it is known to vary as the inverse square of the distance. In fact, what is found to be repeated is always the *relation* of cause and effect, not the cause itself ; all that is necessary as regards the cause is that it should be of the same *kind* (in the relevant respect) as earlier causes whose effects have been observed.

Another respect in which Bergson's statement of causation is inadequate is in its assumption that the cause must be *one* event, whereas it may be two or more events, or even some continuous process. The substantive question at issue is whether mental events are determined by the past. Now in such a case as the repeated reading of a poem, it is obvious that our feelings in reading the poem are most emphatically dependent upon the past, but not upon one single event in the past. All our previous readings of the poem must be included in the cause. But we easily perceive a certain law according to which the effect varies as the previous readings increase in number, and in fact Bergson himself tacitly assumes such a law. We decide at last not to read the poem again, because we know that this time the effect would be boredom. We may not know all the niceties and shades of the boredom we should feel, but we know enough to guide our decision, and the prophecy of boredom is none the less true for being more or less general. Thus the kinds of cases upon which Bergson relies are insufficient to show the impossibility of prediction in the only sense in which prediction has practical or emotional interest. We may therefore leave the consideration of his arguments and address ourselves to the problem directly.

The law of causation, according to which later events can theoretically be predicted by means of earlier events, has often been held to be *a priori*, a necessity of thought, a category without which science would be impossible. These claims seem to me excessive. In certain directions the law has been verified empirically, and in other directions there is no positive evidence against it. But science can use it where it has been found to be true, without being forced into any assumption as to its truth in other fields. We cannot, therefore, feel any *a priori* certainty that causation must apply to human volitions.

The question how far human volitions are subject to causal laws is a purely empirical one. Empirically it seems plain that the great majority of our volitions have causes, but it cannot, on this account, be held necessarily certain that all have causes. There are, however, precisely the same kinds of reasons for regarding it as probable that they all have causes as there are in the case of physical events.

We may suppose—though this is doubtful—that there are laws of correlation of the mental and the physical, in virtue of which, given the state of all the matter in the world, and therefore of all the brains and living organisms, the state of all the minds in the world could be inferred, while conversely the state of all the matter in the world could be inferred if the state of all the minds were given. It is obvious that there is *some* degree of correlation between brain and mind, and it is impossible to say how complete it may be. This, however, is not the point which I wish to elicit. What I wish to urge is that, even if we admit the most extreme claims of determinism and of correlation of mind and brain, still the consequences inimical to what is worth preserving in free will do not follow. The belief that they follow results, I think, entirely from the assimilation of causes to volitions, and from the notion that causes *compel* their effects in some sense analogous to that in which a human authority can compel a man to do what he would rather not do. This assimilation, as soon as the true nature of scientific causal laws is realized, is seen to be a sheer mistake. But this brings us to the second of the two questions which we raised in regard to free will, namely whether, assuming determinism, our actions can be in any proper sense regarded as compelled by outside forces.

(2) *Are human actions subject to an external compulsion?* We have, in deliberation, a subjective sense of freedom, which is sometimes alleged against the view that volitions have causes. This sense of freedom, however, is only a sense that we can choose which we please of a number of alternatives : it does not show us that there is no causal connection between what we please to chose and our previous history. The supposed inconsistency of these two springs from the habit of conceiving causes as analogous to volitions —a habit which often survives unconsciously in those who intend to conceive causes in a more scientific manner. If a cause is analogous to a volition, outside causes will be analogous to an alien will, and acts predictable from outside causes will be subject to compulsion. But this view of cause is one to which science lends no countenance. Causes, we have seen, do not *compel* their effects, any more than effects *compel* their causes. There is a mutual relation, so that either can be inferred from the other. When the geologist infers the past state of the earth from its present state, we should not say that the present state *compels* the past state to have been what it was ; yet it renders it necessary as a consequence of the data, in the only sense in which effects are rendered necessary by their causes. The difference which we *feel*, in this respect, between causes and effects is a

mere confusion due to the fact that we remember past events but do not happen to have memory of the future.

The apparent indeterminateness of the future, upon which some advocates of free will rely, is merely a result of our ignorance. It is plain that no desirable kind of free will can be dependent simply upon our ignorance ; for if that were the case, animals would be more free than men, and savages than civilized people. Free will in any valuable sense must be compatible with the fullest knowledge. Now, quite apart from any assumption as to causality, it is obvious that complete knowledge would embrace the future as well as the past. Our knowledge of the past is not wholly based upon causal inferences, but is partly derived from memory. It is a mere accident that we have no memory of the future. We might—as in the pretended visions of seers—see future events immediately, in the way in which we see past events. They certainly will be what they will be, and are in this sense just as determined as the past. If we saw future events in the same immediate way in which we see past events, what kind of free will would still be possible ? Such a kind would be wholly independent of determinism : it could not be contrary to even the most entirely universal reign of causality. And such a kind must contain whatever is worth having in free will, since it is impossible to believe that mere ignorance can be the essential condition of any good thing. Let us therefore imagine a set of beings who know the whole future with absolute certainty, and let us ask ourselves whether they could have anything that we should call free will.

Such beings as we are imagining would not have to wait for the event in order to know what decision they were going to adopt on some future occasion. They would know now what their volitions were going to be. But would they have any reason to regret this knowledge ? Surely not, unless the foreseen volitions were in themselves regrettable. And it is less likely that the foreseen volitions would be regrettable if the steps which would lead to them were also foreseen. It is difficult not to suppose that what is foreseen is fated, and must happen however much it may be dreaded. But human actions are the outcome of desire, and no foreseeing can be true unless it takes account of desire. A foreseen volition will have to be one which does not become odious through being foreseen. The beings we are imagining would easily come to know the causal connections of volitions, and therefore their volitions would be better calculated to satisfy their desires than ours are. Since volitions are the outcome of desires, a prevision of volitions contrary to desires could not be a true one. It must be remembered that the supposed prevision would not create the future any more than memory creates the past. We do not think we were necessarily not free in the past, merely because we can now remember our past volitions. Similarly, we might be free in the future, even if we could now see what our future volitions were going to be. Freedom, in short, in any valuable sense, demands only that our volitions shall be, as they are, the result of our own desires, not of an outside force compelling us to will what we would rather not will. Everything else is confusion of thought, due to the feeling that knowledge *compels* the happening of what it knows when this is future, though it is at once obvious that knowledge has no such power in regard to the past. Free will, therefore, is true in the only form which is important ; and the desire for other forms is a mere effect of insufficient analysis.

What has been said on philosophical method in the foregoing lectures has been rather by means of illustrations in particular cases than by means of general precepts. Nothing of any value can be said on method except through examples ; but now, at the end of our course, we may collect certain general maxims which may possibly be a help in acquiring a philosophical habit of mind and a guide in looking for solutions of philosophic problems.

Philosophy does not become scientific by making use of other sciences, in the kind of way in which, e.g. Herbert Spencer does. Philosophy aims at what is *general*, and the special sciences, however they may *suggest* large generalizations, cannot make them certain. And a hasty generalization, such as Spencer's generalization of evolution, is none the less hasty because what is generalized is the latest scientific theory. Philosophy is a study apart from the other sciences : its results cannot be established by the other sciences, and conversely must not be such as some other science might conceivably contradict. Prophecies as to the future of the universe, for example, are not the business of philosophy ; whether the universe is progressive, retrograde, or stationary, it is not for the philosopher to say.

In order to become a scientific philosopher, a certain peculiar mental discipline is required. There must be present, first of all, the desire to know philosophical truth, and this desire must be sufficiently strong to survive through years when there seems no hope of its finding any satisfaction. The desire to know philosophical truth is very rare—in its purity, it is not often found even among philosophers. It is obscured sometimes—particularly after long periods of fruitless search—by the desire to *think* we know. Some plausible opinion presents itself, and by turning our attention away from the objections to it, or merely by not making great efforts to find objections to it, we may obtain the comfort of believing it, although, if we had resisted the wish for comfort, we should have come to see that the opinion was false. Again the desire for unadulterated truth is often obscured, in professional philosophers, by love of system : the one little fact which will not come inside the philosopher's edifice has to be pushed and tortured until it seems to consent. Yet the one little fact is more likely to be important for the future than the system with which it is inconsistent. Pythagoras invented a system which fitted admirably with all the facts he knew, except the incommensurability of the diagonal of a square and the side ; this one little fact stood out, and remained a fact even after Hippasos of Metapontion was drowned for revealing it. To us, the discovery of this fact is the chief claim of Pythagoras to immortality, while his system has become a matter of merely historical curiosity.[1] Love of system, therefore, and the system-maker's vanity which becomes associated with it, are among the snares that the student of philosophy must guard against.

The desire to establish this or that result, or generally to discover evidence for agreeable results, of whatever kind, has of course been the chief obstacle to honest philosophizing. So strangely perverted do men become by unrecognized passions, that a determination in

---

[1] The above remarks, for purposes of illustration, adopt one of several possible opinions on each of several disputed points.

advance to arrive at this or that conclusion is generally regarded as a mark of virtue, and those whose studies lead to an opposite conclusion are thought to be wicked. No doubt it is commoner to wish to arrive at an agreeable result than to wish to arrive at a true result. But only those in whom the desire to arrive at a *true* result is paramount can hope to serve any good purpose by the study of philosophy.

But even when the desire to know exists in the requisite strength, the mental vision by which abstract truth is recognized is hard to distinguish from vivid imaginability and consonance with mental habits. It is necessary to practise methodological doubt, like Descartes, in order to loosen the hold of mental habits ; and it is necessary to cultivate logical imagination, in order to have a number of hypotheses at command, and not to be the slave of the one which common sense has rendered easy to imagine. These two processes, of doubting the familiar and imagining the unfamiliar, are correlative, and form the chief part of the mental training required for a philosopher.

The naïve beliefs which we find in ourselves when we first begin the process of philosophic reflection may turn out, in the end, to be almost all capable of a true interpretation ; but they ought all, before being admitted into philosophy, to undergo the ordeal of sceptical criticism. Until they have gone through this ordeal, they are mere blind habits, ways of behaving rather than intellectual convictions. And although it may be that a majority will pass the test, we may be pretty sure that some will not, and that a serious readjustment of our outlook ought to result. In order to break the dominion of habit, we must do our best to doubt the senses, reason, morals, everything in short. In some directions, doubt will be found possible ; in others, it will be checked by that direct vision of abstract truth upon which the possibility of philosophical knowledge depends.

At the same time, and as an essential aid to the direct perception of the truth, it is necessary to acquire fertility in imagining abstract hypotheses. This is, I think, what has most of all been lacking hitherto in philosophy. So meagre was the logical apparatus that all the hypotheses philosophers could imagine were found to be inconsistent with the facts. Too often this state of things led to the adoption of heroic measures, such as a wholesale denial of the facts, when an imagination better stocked with logical tools would have found a key to unlock the mystery. It is in this way that the study of logic becomes the central study in philosophy : it gives the method of research in philosophy, just as mathematics gives the method in physics. And as physics, which, from Plato to the Renaissance, was as unprogressive, dim, and superstitious as philosophy, became a science through Galileo's fresh observation of facts and subsequent mathematical manipulation, so philosophy, in our own day, is becoming scientific through the simultaneous acquisition of new facts and logical methods.

In spite, however, of the new possibility of progress in philosophy, the first effect, as in the case of physics, is to diminish very greatly the extent of what is thought to be known. Before Galileo, people believed themselves possessed of immense knowledge on all the most interesting questions in physics. He established certain facts as to the way in which bodies fall, not very interesting on their own account, but of quite immeasurable interest as examples of real knowledge and of a new method whose future fruitfulness he himself divined. But his few facts sufficed to destroy the whole vast system of supposed knowledge handed down from Aristotle, as even the palest morning sun suffices to extinguish the stars. So in philosophy : though some have believed one system, and others another, almost all have been of opinion that a great deal was known ; but all this supposed knowledge in the traditional systems must be swept away, and a new beginning must be made, which we shall esteem fortunate indeed if it can attain results comparable to Galileo's law of falling bodies.

By the practice of methodological doubt, if it is genuine and prolonged, a certain humility as to our knowledge is induced : we become glad to know *anything* in philosophy, however seemingly trivial. Philosophy has suffered from the lack of this kind of modesty. It has made the mistake of attacking the interesting problems at once, instead of proceeding patiently and slowly, accumulating whatever solid knowledge was obtainable, and trusting the great problems to the future. Men of science are not ashamed of what is intrinsically trivial, if its consequences are likely to be important ; the *immediate* outcome of an experiment is hardly ever interesting on its own account. So in philosophy, it is often desirable to expend time and care on matters which, judged alone, might seem frivolous, for it is often only through the consideration of such matters that the greater problems can be approached.

When our problem has been selected, and the necessary mental discipline has been acquired, the method to be pursued is fairly uniform. The big problems which provoke philosophical inquiry are found, on examination, to be complex, and to depend upon a number of component problems, usually more abstract than those of which they are the components.

It will generally be found that all our initial data, all
the facts that we seem to know to begin with, suffer
from vagueness, confusion, and complexity. Current
philosophical ideas share these defects ; it is therefore
necessary to create an apparatus of precise conceptions
as general and as free from complexity as possible,
before the data can be analysed into the kind of
premises which philosophy aims at discovering. In
this process of analysis, the source of difficulty is
tracked further and further back, growing at each
stage more abstract, more refined, more difficult to
apprehend. Usually it will be found that a number
of these extraordinarily abstract questions underlie
any one of the big obvious problems. When everything has been done that can be done by method, a
stage is reached where only direct philosophic vision
can carry matters further. Here only genius will
avail. What is wanted, as a rule, is some new effort
of logical imagination, some glimpse of a possibility
never conceived before, and then the direct perception
that this possibility is realized in the case in question.
Failure to think of the right possibility leaves insoluble
difficulties, balanced arguments pro and con, utter
bewilderment and despair. But the right possibility,
as a rule, when once conceived, justifies itself swiftly
by its astonishing power of absorbing apparently
conflicting facts. From this point onward, the work
of the philosopher is synthetic and comparatively easy ;
it is in the very last stage of the analysis that the real
difficulty consists.

Of the prospect of progress in philosophy, it would
be rash to speak with confidence. Many of the
traditional problems of philosophy, perhaps most of
those which have interested a wider circle than that
of technical students, do not appear to be soluble by

scientific methods. Just as astronomy lost much of its human interest when it ceased to be astrology, so philosophy must lose in attractiveness as it grows less prodigal of promises. But to the large and still growing body of men engaged in the pursuit of science —men who hitherto, not without justification, have turned aside from philosophy with a certain contempt —the new method, successful already in such time-honoured problems as number, infinity, continuity, space and time, should make an appeal which the older methods have wholly failed to make. Physics, with its principle of relativity and its revolutionary investigations into the nature of matter, is feeling the need for that kind of novelty in fundamental hypotheses which scientific philosophy aims at facilitating. The one and only condition, I believe, which is necessary in order to secure for philosophy in the near future an achievement surpassing all that has hitherto been accomplished by philosophers, is the creation of a school of men with scientific training and philosophical interests, unhampered by the traditions of the past, and not misled by the literary methods of those who copy the ancients in all except their merits.

INDEX

GEORGE ALLEN & UNWIN LTD

Head Office:
London: 40 Museum Street, W.C.1

Sales, Distribution and Accounts Departments:
Park Lane, Hemel Hempstead, Herts

Argentina: Rodriguez Pena 1653–11B, Buenos Aires
Australia: Cnr. Bridge Road and Jersey Street, Hornsby, N.S.W. 2077
Canada: 2330 Midland Avenue, Agincourt, Ontario
Greece: 7 Stadiou Street, Athens 125
India: 103/5 Fort Street, Bombay 1
285J Bepin Behari Ganguli Street, Calcutta 12
2/18 Mount Road, Madras 2
4/21–22B Asaf Ali Road, New Delhi 1
Japan: 29/13 Hongo 5 Chome, Bunkyo, Tokyo 113
Kenya: P.O. Box 30583, Nairobi
Lebanon: Deeb Building, Jeanne d'Arc Street, Beirut
Mexico: Serapio Rendon 125, Mexico 4, D.F.
New Zealand: 46 Lake Road, Northcote, Auckland 9
Nigeria: P.O. Box 62, Ibadan
Pakistan: Karachi Chambers, McLeod Road, Karachi 2
22 Falettis' Hotel, Egerton Road, Lahore
Philippines: 3 Malaming Street, U.P. Village, Quezon City, D-505
Singapore: 248c/1 Orchard Road, Singapore 9
South Africa: P.O. Box 23134, Joubert Park, Johannesburg
West Indies: Rockley New Road, St. Lawrence 4, Barbados

By Bertrand Russell

HUMAN KNOWLEDGE:

ITS SCOPES AND LIMITS   *Demy 8vo.*

This book is intended for the general reader, not for professional philosophers. It begins with a brief survey of what science professes to know about the universe. In this survey the attempt is to be as far as possible impartial and impersonal; the aim is to come as near as our capacities permit to describing the world as it might appear to an observer of miraculous perceptive powers viewing it from without. In science, we are concerned with what we *know* rather than what *we* know. We attempt to use an order in our description which ignores, for the moment, the fact that we are part of the universe, and that any account which we can give of it depends upon its effects upon ourselves, and is to this extent inevitably anthropocentric.

Bertrand Russell accordingly begins with the system of galaxies, and passes on, by stages, to our own galaxy, our own little solar system, our own tiny planet, the infinitesimal specks of life upon its surface, and finally, as the climax of insignificance, the bodies and minds of those odd beings that imagine themselves the lords of creation and the end of the whole vast cosmos.

But this survey, which seems to end in the pettiness of Man and all his concerns, is only one side of the truth. There is another side, which must be brought out by a survey of a different kind. In this second kind of survey, the question is no longer what the universe is, but how we come to know whatever we do know about it. In this survey Man again occupies the centre, as in the Ptolemaic astronomy. What we know of the world we know by means of events in our own lives, events which, but for the power of thought, would remain merely private.

The book inquires what are our data, and what are the principles by means of which we make our inferences. The data from which these inferences proceed are private to ourselves; what we call "seeing the sun" is an event in the life of the seer, from which the astronomer's sun has to be inferred by a long and elaborate process. It is evident that, if the world were a higgledy-piggledy chaos, inferences of this kind would be impossible; but for casual inter-connectedness, what happens in one place would afford no indication of what has happened in another. It is the process from private sensation and thought to impersonal science that forms the chief topic of the book. The road is at times difficult, but until we have traversed it neither the scope nor the limitations of human knowledge can be adequately understood.

HISTORY OF WESTERN PHILOSOPHY

916 pages.   *Demy 8vo.*

"It is certain of a very wide audience, and is, in my opinion, just the kind of thing people ought to have to make them understand the past. . . . It may be one of the most valuable books of our time."

Dr. G. M. TREVELYAN

"Bertrand Russell's remarkable book is, so far as I am aware, the first attempt to present a history of western philosophy in relation to its social and economic background. As such, and also as a brilliantly written exposé of changing philosophical doctrines, it should be widely read."

Dr. JULIAN HUXLEY, F.R.S.

"A survey of western philosophy in relation to its environment, of such sweep and acuteness, alive in every nerve, is a masterpiece of intellectual energy . . . the Socrates of our time."

A. L. ROWSE

"By any reckoning a great book."

C. E. M. JOAD in *The Fortnightly Review*

"The best history of philosophy in English."

Life and Letters

POWER: A NEW SOCIAL ANALYSIS

Crown 8vo.

Many readers consider this to be Bertrand Russell's most important book. The present reprint is timely.

Russell's purpose in *Power* was to prove that the fundamental concept in social science is Power, in the same sense in which Energy is the fundamental concept in physics. Like energy, power has many forms, especially military, economic, and propaganda forms. None is fundamental; none can be subordinated to other forms; none can be adequately studied in isolation. The laws of social dynamics can only be treated in terms of power in general, not of any one form, e.g. the economic.

The book first enumerates forms of power; then considers various historical examples of the evolution of power, especially monarchy and theocracy, then examines the basis of power in individual psychology, and certain philosophers which are actuated by power motives. Finally, it examines the relation of power to human welfare, and the problem of the taming of power.

THE ANALYSIS OF MIND

Demy 8vo.

"Brilliant . . . one of the most interesting and important books that Mr. Russell has yet given us." *Nation*

"Here are the old clarity and the old charm; the restrained, illuminating wit . . . a most brilliant essay in psychology." *New Statesman*

"Most interesting . . . a most valuable contribution to its subject." *Manchester Guardian*

"This interesting and fascinating book . . . is a perfect model of what such books should be . . . the style is so clear and technicalities so carefully explained that the reading of the book is an intellectual pleasure rather than a mental effort." *Church Times*

THE PRINCIPLES OF MATHEMATICS

Small Royal 8vo.

THE PRINCIPLES OF MATHEMATICS, first published in 1903, sets forth, as far as possible without mathematical or logic symbolism, the grounds in favour of the view that mathematics and logic are identical, what is commonly called mathematics being merely later deductions from logical premisses. The detailed proof of this thesis was subsequently given by Professor Whitehead and the present author in PRINCIPIA MATHEMATICA; in the "Principles" it is defended against such advance philosophical opinions as were at that time current. It has since been attacked, and in a new Preface the author defends his thesis against adverse opinions.